MW01104994

Child Abuse:
What You
Can Do About It

Angela R. Carl

Child Abuse: What You Can Do About It

Angela R. Carl

COLLEGE PRESS
PUBLISHING COMPANY
Joplin, Missouri

Printed and Bound in the
United States of America

International Standard Book Number: 0-89900-462-8

Dedicated with love to:

my precious daughters *Cassandra*, *Anya*, and *Lucinda* for their love and affection,

my husband *Ed* for his enthusiastic support and patience,

my own nurturing parents and brothers, *Steve* and *Dale*, who taught me about God's unconditional love.

Table of Contents

FOREWORD

Reports of sexual abuse of children in day-care centers, schools, and other child-frequented places have zigzagged across the nation in recent years.

Dozens of stories from every state in the country have been sensationalized by the press and have contributed to an escalating mass hysteria on the part of many. The "best-kept-secret" of child sexual abuse has become one of today's parents' greatest concerns.

Despite increased awareness of the prevalence of the problem, many misconceptions about child sexual abuse linger on. During the past two decades, experts have learned a great deal about its nature, causes, effects, and treatments. Many human service agencies and organizations have focused on educating the public about the dynamics of the problem. The alarm has been sounded, the public has been outraged, and the nation has become committed to working toward its prevention.

Oddly enough, a number of sociologists and psychologists have asked, "Where is the church? We don't see many Christian groups in the forefront of the battle against child abuse." This attitude was reflected by Dr. Jon Conte, professor and researcher from the University of Chicago. Addressing leaders in the field at a conference in New York on the prevention of child sexual exploitation Dr. Conte asserted, "Churches have largely ignored child sexual victimization."[1]

In outlining prevention strategies, Dr. Conte included the need to instruct children about personal body safety. Many schools now include sexual abuse prevention lessons in their curriculums. Such wide-scale instruction is necessary in order to reach *all* children, as many are abused within their own homes. However, as Dr. Conte emphasized, "The *best* place for such instruction is from families, churches, and synagogues." Churches and families provide a better setting than schools since the teaching of values, interpersonal relationship skills, and skills for abuse prevention need to be reinforced and expanded over a long period of time.

Of course, *many* Christians and *some* churches have addressed the problem of child abuse. But Dr. Conte's assertions underline the general consensus among sociologists that churches are in a position to do a great deal more.

As a Christian committed to advocating for the rights and well-being of children, I feel compelled to call upon other Christians to respond not only to the crime of child sexual victimization, but also to the other forms of child abuse, including physical and emotional maltreatment and neglect.

The first part of this book emphasizes the problem of child sexual abuse, and it is intended to help anyone involved with children to better understand the problem. An accurate understanding of the problem is necessary in order to teach children the knowledge and skills they need to protect themselves from sexual abuse.

The information included will no doubt arouse uncomfortable feelings, emotions, and perhaps memories. We like to believe that childhood is a carefree time for innocence and fun. It is most upsetting to realize that "good" children are especially vulnerable to sexual assault. Yet, in truth, children are totally controlled by adults who have unlimited power over them. When sin rears its ugly head, adults do all kinds of things contrary to God's perfect plan for mankind. Innocent, untrained children are powerless to defend themselves against the consequences of an adult's sinful behavior. It is up to adults who love them to do everything possible to protect them from harm.

Hopefully, an increased understanding of child sexual abuse will help readers to clearly and sensitively communicate personal safety information to the children they love.

If we are serious about preventing child abuse, we need to go beyond sexual abuse prevention education. Trying to keep something "bad" from happening to our own children isn't enough. We must also try to make something "good" happen for many children and parents. The "positive approach" for primary prevention of abuse promoted by the National Committee for Prevention of Child Abuse calls for increased efforts to *enhance* parent-child relationships for the population at large. Being a parent is not easy, and most individuals assume this responsibility with little or no training! Since it would be impossible to single out all potentially abusive parents, we need to direct efforts toward *all* parents. Besides, what parent isn't abusive in some way or at least *feels* abusive on occasion? We all have moments of exasperation when we would like to lock our children away in a closet for a few hours! If more parents are taught *how* to parent, and are provided with more support and help, reason the experts, the incidence of child abuse will certainly decrease![2]

For long-term abuse prevention, children need better preparation for their roles as future adults and parents. Beginning with increased emphasis on developing good interpersonal relationships and a sense of self-worth, parents and teachers can help children learn the skills and attitudes essential for positive family interactions. Specific parenting education should be provided for adolescents and young adults *before* they become parents.

The effects of child abuse directly impact every citizen in the nation. The cycle is self-perpetuating, and many abused children pursue paths of violence and other criminal activities. Many victims remain emotionally disturbed for the rest of their lives. This enormous problem of society can only be solved by an enormous effort. Large-scale, state-funded programs are needed to provide short-term assistance for child victims and their parents. But abuse prevention cannot be achieved without dedicated volunteers who are willing to put their concern and compassion into action.

Let's not sit back waiting for "someone else" to put an end to child abuse. Who could be better suited to help parents and children understand what love really means than God's own children? An added benefit for parents who help others learn how to parent is that they become better parents themselves! Chapters 8 and 9 provide a number of specific suggestions for abuse prevention which Christians can help effect in their own communities and churches. Let's show the world how God values children and parents!

A unified Christian effort *will* make a difference!

Angela R. Carl

CHAPTER ONE

What's a Parent to Do?

Children are . . .

What thoughts come to your mind when you read this phrase? Obviously, there are many ways to describe children, and your response may vary with the time of day, your mood, the season, and the amount of experience you have had with little ones.

Consider these Biblical passages:

"Children are a heritage of the Lord; and the fruit of the womb is his reward. As arrows are in the hand of a mighty man; so are children of the youth. Happy is the man that hath his quiver full of them" (Psalm 127:3-5).

"For you created my inmost being; you knit me together in my mother's womb. I praise you because I am fearfully and wonderfully made; your works are wonderful, I know that full

well" (Psalm 139:13,14, NIV).

Jesus said, *"Whoever welcomes this little child in my name welcomes me"* (Luke 9:48, NIV).

Jesus said, *"Let the little children come to me, and do not hinder them, for the kingdom of God belongs to such as these. I tell you the truth, anyone who will not receive the kingdom of God like a little child will never enter it. And he took the children in his arms, put his hands on them and blessed them"* (Mark 10:14-16, NIV).

Read about the joy of Abraham and Sarah when they learned they were to be blessed with a son in their "golden years" (Genesis 17:15-21; 21:1-8). God blessed Job after his prolonged troubles by giving him seven sons and three daughters (Job 42:13).

These are only a few examples of Biblical references to children.

Children are . . .
   a gift from God and a great source of happiness for their parents.
Children are . . .
   vulnerable, dependent, powerless, in need of protection and care.

Accompanying the joy of parenthood is the tremendous responsibility of providing care and instruction for children.

Old Testament Scriptures stressed parents' responsibility to spend much time teaching their children the commandments of the Lord (Deuteronomy 6:7).

"Train a child in the way he should go, and when he is old he will not turn from it" (Proverbs 22:6, NIV).

Jesus' teaching in Matthew 18:2-5 emphasizes the impor-

14

tance of protecting children from harm. The passage clearly indicates how God values little ones. Those who possess the qualities of humility and innocence found in little children will occupy a position of greatness in God's kingdom. In God's eyes, a child's value lies not in his achievements or his good behavior but in himself.

Jesus does not even name the punishment that will be meted out to those who harm children, but it is surely something worse than death! **"Whoever causes one of these little ones who believe in Me to stumble, it is better for him that a heavy millstone be hung around his neck, and that he be drowned in the depth of the sea"** (Matthew 18:6, NAS).

Jesus' lesson about greatness in God's kingdom provides a tremendous motivation to advocate more forcefully for children's rights!

Ephesians 6:1-4 speaks to both children and parents. A child is to obey his parents, but parents must be careful not to exasperate their children.

Most God-fearing parents gratefully accept this responsibility. They begin teaching their children at an early age what is needed to get along in the world as well as what is needed to please God. They repeat endless bits of advice to their youngsters to make certain the messages sink in. Indeed, many children could recite these "parent tapes" in their sleep! The following string of admonitions echo through many young heads:

- Don't touch a hot stove.
- Look both ways before crossing the street.
- Never touch an electrical outlet.
- Never play with matches.
- Don't drink from bottles marked with a skull and crossbones.

15

Since the dangers involved are clear, preventive precautions are clear. Well-informed parents explain the specific consequences of the dangers so their children understand the full implication of not heeding their admonitions. A warning about an additional danger is usually included in the list of dos and don'ts. This "parent tape" may be phrased, *"Watch out for strangers,"* or *"Don't talk to strangers."* This danger is a bit muddier and parents are often reluctant to explain to their children just what the consequences might be. As a result, children frequently do not really comprehend the "stranger danger."

First of all, *exactly who is a stranger?* What about the man who says "Hi, there, aren't you Jack's daughter? I work with your daddy." The helpful child may reply, "No, my daddy's name is Eric." "Oh, that's right," laughs the man. "Your dad and I go out for lunch all the time. He tells me all about you. He says you just love bubble gum. I was on my way to buy some. Hey, I'll buy you a pack. Come with me and you can choose your favorite flavor. Your dad will be glad I saw you. I'll bring you right back." A skilled individual can win the trust of a vulnerable child very easily. Before long, the person is not a *stranger*, but a *friend*.

Even if the term *stranger* has been well defined, the child may not have any idea *why* strangers should be avoided. *What might they do? What should the child do if a stranger tries to take him away?* With no concept of what to do in the worst case, a child's imagination about the unknown may create an overwhelming fear of strangers. For some youngsters the term "stranger" has the same connotation as "boogeyman" had for the last generation, and may be the subject for nightmares and anxiety.

Don't Frighten! Enlighten!

The media's extensive coverage of incidents of child sexual abuse has contributed to a gnawing fear that no child is safe outside his parents' sight. Some parents have reacted by frightening their children. They refuse to allow even older children to play alone in the yard or to walk to a friend's home down the street. Certainly precautions are wise, but prudence must be exercised so that a child does not feel as though he is wearing a leash! The development of a child's independence will be thwarted if he is overprotected. Not only is overprotection unhealthy for both children and parents, but it is also impractical! It is virtually impossible for a child to spend every waking moment under the wings of his parents.

Rather, parents can turn their anxiety into informed understanding of the problem of child sexual abuse. They can develop some sensible prevention strategies with their children.

All children should have knowledge of how to deal with strangers who might approach them. Strategies for teaching self-protection skills to children are included in the teaching guide. However it is a well-known fact that *at least 85% of child sexual abuse is committed by individuals who are known and trusted by the children.* Prevention skills must also include ways to handle situations of potential abuse from adults and adolescents children know. Children who know what to expect are less vulnerable to sexual abuse than are those who have never been given this important information. Once children are empowered with knowledge about personal body safety, they will be much better equipped to handle a situation of potential abuse. They will know what to do if it does happen to them.

In some respects, teaching children about personal body safety is similar to teaching water safety. Children need to understand what can happen in deep water if they cannot swim. Yet they will not learn to enjoy the water if they become overly fearful of drowning. Thus, parents try to communicate a healthy caution about deep water with some very specific guidelines about how to avoid trouble and what to do to keep afloat. Also, most parents try to see that their children learn to swim.

Similarly, because all children are potential victims of child sexual abuse, they need to be told the reality of the danger on a level they can understand. At the same time, they need to learn to enjoy making new acquaintances and to draw from the experiences of the adults they know. Parents do not want their children to distrust everyone they come in contact with, nor to recoil with fear every time a friendly adult touches them. They want to encourage them to grow through interactions with other individuals.

"But *how* can I teach my child to be on guard without causing him to become paranoid about every stranger or adult who looks his way?" protest frustrated parents. "It's impossible to accomplish both needs!" Actually, children can handle information about sexuality and abuse far better than most adults give them credit for. First, parents need to reassure their youngsters that *most* adults like children and do not wish to harm them. After full discussion about the positive aspects of relationships with adults, children should be given permission to trust their feelings when they sense that something is wrong. They need to be empowered with the knowledge that their bodies belong to them, and that they can stand up for themselves if *anyone* tries to abuse them. With knowledge about personal body safety, children can feel more confident

18

about interactions with adults as well as school bullies! *(Suggestions for discussions are included in the second part of this book.)*

This book is intended to meet three primary needs:
(1) *to acquaint parents, teachers, ministers, counselors, and others who work with children with the problem of child sexual abuse and what they can do about it;*
(2) *to offer suggested ways in which Christians can help alleviate the problem of child abuse and neglect in general and reduce the risk of abuse occurring within their own church;*
(3) *to provide specific guidelines for teaching children personal body safety from a Christian perspective.*
The teaching section is designed for use with the pupil's activity book.

Note: The gender used to designate a singular child varies throughout the book. This gender change is intentional and interchangeable as both boys and girls are at equal risk of sexual abuse. It is also understood that sexual abusers may be either male or female.

CHAPTER TWO

What Exactly Is Child Abuse?

Humpty Dumpty sat on a wall,
Humpty Dumpty had a great fall;
All the King's horses and all the King's men
Couldn't put Humpty Dumpty together again.

If the rescue squad were called out for Humpty Dumpty today, several questions might be asked. *Why did Humpty fall? Could one of his parents have pushed him during a fit of anger? Did he lose his balance while in a state of overwhelming emotional depression? Had his mother allowed him to play at a dangerous construction site? Or was his fall simply a terrible "childhood accident"?*

Although signs of child abuse and neglect are often glaringly obvious, it is sometimes very difficult to ascertain whether or not a child's injury or disturbed emotional state is the result of abuse. Children who have been abused often suffer effects equally as devastating as Humpty Dumpty did. Even the best efforts by psychiatrists, social workers, and other supportive adults can seldom put a child totally together again after he has been torn apart.

Definitions of abuse and neglect are based on the assumption that children are dependent upon adults for survival and appropriate socialization.

> **Child abuse is damage to a child for which there is no "reasonable" explanation.** *In general, abuse and neglect refer to specific acts of commission or omission by parents or other adults responsible for children under eighteen that lead to nonaccidental harm or threatened harm to a child's physical, mental, or emotional developmental state.* Forms of child abuse are usually identified as *sexual abuse, physical abuse, emotional maltreatment, and neglect.*

Sexual Abuse

For many, the term *child sexual abuse* calls to mind an image of a pitiful, trembling child wearing torn clothing, covered with bruises and blood. This image is based on the gruesome reality that sometimes children are violently raped and even murdered. Indeed, the very idea of an adult forcing a child to have sexual intercourse is revolting. In actual fact, most child victims show no outward physical signs of abuse. Child sexual abuse includes a much larger scope of sexual behavior than forcible intercourse.

There are many different interpretations of exactly what constitutes child sexual abuse, and, unfortunately, definitions vary greatly in different state laws and penal codes.

The crackdown on sexual abuse by local law enforcement agencies has caused an overreaction on the part of some child workers and parents. Some have become so fearful of being accused of child molesting that they have stopped hugging children! Concerned parents have indicated that they feel uncomfortable even bathing the genitals of their young children. Some baby sitters have refused to change toddlers' diapers to avoid any chance of being accused of sexual abuse. Thus, it is important to reassure child caretakers what kinds of behaviors are *not* sexually abusive, as well as those that *are.*

Fond or playful expressions of love and affection between adults and children are *not* child sexual abuse. "Good touches" are important as they often communicate feelings of love in a way that words or deeds cannot. Responsible adults automatically limit their physical exchanges with children to those expressions of warm, healthy, affectionate feelings that are appropriate for their relationship.

Neither is it considered to be abusive when a health professional, parent, or other person caring for a child administers medical care to the child's genitalia. And bathing and powdering a young child's genitals is necessary for good personal hygiene!

Sexual abuse is the exploitation of a child under eighteen by an adult or older child *(at least four years older than the victim)* for the purpose of the perpetrator's sexual gratification.

The perpetrator *(abuser)* typically holds a position of power over the victim, thus enabling the abuse to continue.

Dr. Gary May, a child psychiatrist, separates sexual offenses into two general categories: *nontouching* and *touching offenses.*[3]

Nontouching offenses include

- verbal sexual stimulation intended to arouse the child's interest, or shock him,
- obscene telephone calls,
- exhibitionism *(indecent exposure)* (**Note:** *This does not include nudity within a household unless it is for the purpose of an adult's sexual gratification from the child.*),
- voyeurism *(peeping in doors and windows),* and
- primal scene *(causing or allowing a child to witness adults having sexual relations).* (**Note:** *If this occurs accidentally, it is not considered to be sexual abuse. Parents should reassure the child witness that love is good and not harmful, and talk openly with the child about his feelings. Young children might think "daddy is hurting mommy" or vice versa if the situation is not explained.*)

Touching offenses include

- nonviolent touches such as fondling,
- oral, genital, or anal stimulation and penetration,
- nonviolent intercourse,
- incest,
- violent, forcible offenses of rape, physical injury, assault, and murder.

Child sexual abuse also includes

- coercion of the child by the perpetrator to touch or look at him for the purpose of his sexual gratification, and
- the exploitation of children through pornography and prostitution.

Incest refers to sexual relationships between blood relatives who would be prohibited by law from marrying.

Other terms used synonymously with child sexual abuse include *child molestation, sexual exploitation, sexual mistreatment or maltreatment,* and *sexual assault. Sexual offenders* are referred to as *molesters, rapists, abusers, perpetrators,* and *pedophiles.*

Although the definitions of child abuse in state laws vary it is illegal in all fifty states of the United States to sexually abuse a child, even if the child seemed to consent to the sexual activity. Many state legislatures are adding amendments to their laws to make a greater scope of sexual behaviors against children punishable crimes.

Physical Abuse

> **Nonaccidental physical injuries or acts that create a substantial risk of serious injury that are inflicted or allowed to be inflicted by a child's caretaker are categorized as physical abuse.**

Injuries may be caused by beating, biting, pinching, binding, pulling hair, burning, branding, punching, shaking, and slapping. Physical assault may be inflicted with an implement such as a knife, strap, belt buckle, rope, cigarette, or without an implement. A rough shove that causes a child to fall and become injured may be considered physical abuse if the resulting injury is severe. Bruises in various stages of healing can be a clue that a child is being physically abused. Overdisciplining or using punishments that are inappropriate for the child's age or condition can also be forms of physical abuse.

"Reasonable" corporal punishment (spanking) is *not* considered child abuse, as physical discipline is considered part of parents' rights in rearing their children. Christian parents who believe in spanking know Proverbs 13:24 by heart! *"He who spares the rod hates his son, but he who loves him is careful to discipline him."* (NIV) However "excessive" corporal punishment may be considered abusive or neglectful.

Where is the line drawn between the use of a physical punishment as a disciplinary action *(slapping, spanking or hitting, for example)* and physical abuse? It is not always clear by any means, but most authorities consider **marks such as bruises, lacerations, scars, or welts left on a child's body over forty-eight hours an indication that a child has been physically harmed.**

The following guidelines can be used to help determine whether or not a punishment was "reasonable":

- What was the purpose of the punishment? To train or discipline a child or to satisfy a parent's need to express anger?
- Was the punishment appropriate? Was it too severe for the child's age or understanding level? Was the severity of the punishment in line with the misbehavior of the child? Could a less severe punishment have been equally effective?
- Was the punishment brutal or beyond the child's capacity to endure? If physical force was used, where was it applied? *(Buttocks and thighs are reasonably safe areas of the body but the head and genitalia are not.)*

Injuries are commonly explained as accidental by abusive parents and fearful child victims. Thus teachers and medical personnel are being trained to carefully examine bruises and marks, and to try to determine whether or not the explanation sounds plausible in light of the injury and conditions surrounding it.

Emotional Maltreatment

> **Emotional Maltreatment is defined as a pattern of blaming, belittling, verbally attacking, or rejecting a child, or demanding that a child assume responsibilities that he is incapable of handling. A persistent lack of concern for a child's welfare is also considered emotional maltreatment.**

In general, emotional maltreatment is indicated by a substantial impairment of a child's emotional or intellectual capability as a result of acts of commission or omission by the caretaker as previously described.

This form of abuse is the most difficult to prove as most parents are guilty of some emotionally abusive behavior at one time or another and a certain amount of emotional abuse is accepted by society. For some parents, though, emotional maltreatment of their children becomes *a pattern of life* as opposed to an occasional frustrated outburst followed by an apology and expression of love. Often one child in a family is singled out as a scapegoat for all the family's problems. Children who are mentally retarded, physically handicapped, or have other special needs that make them difficult to manage sometimes become targets of emotional abuse. Babies who "fail to thrive" through a lack of mothering are often considered to be victims of emotional abuse.

An emotionally disturbed child may exhibit behaviors similar to a maltreated child. This causes difficulty in determining the underlying cause of the child's problems. A distinguishing factor is the difference in parental behavior. While an emotionally disturbed child's parents are usually concerned about his welfare, and seek professional help for him, maltreating parents often blame the child for the problem and refuse offers of help. Ordinarily, effects of maltreatment must be severe enough to constitute a handicap before a parent is charged with emotional abuse. While emotional maltreatment does occur alone, it almost always accompanies physical abuse and sometimes sexual abuse and neglect.

Neglect

Neglectful caretakers do not exercise even a bare minimum degree. of care in providing food, clothing, shelter, medical care, education, and supervision.

The greatest number of child maltreatment reports are for this form of abuse. Charges of neglect do not refer to subjective judgments about an individual's child-rearing practices or differing cultural expectations and values.

All children skip meals, wear soiled or torn clothing, go to school with runny noses, and experience accidents that might have been prevented by parents from time to time. But **neglect involves a chronic inattention to the basic needs of a child.**

Examples of neglect are numerous. Parents who abuse drugs or alcohol may be charged with neglect when their impaired condition causes or could cause direct harm to their child's physical, emotional, or mental development. Allowing a child to ride in a car with an intoxicated driver should be regarded as child neglect. Parents who knowingly allow siblings or underage children in a household to abuse a younger child sexually are often charged with neglect. Likewise, parents who knowingly permit a child to engage in delinquency or serious drug or alcohol abuse are legally neglectful.

One of the most frequently reported charges of neglect is educational neglect by parents who permit chronic school truancy, or fail to enroll a child in school.

The provision of basic needs is based on a minimum standard of care available to even the most impoverished families through public assistance. If parents who are reported as neglectful indicate they cannot afford to care for their children, they will usually be offered services and needed assistance.

CHAPTER THREE

Is Child Abuse a Twentieth Century Phenomenon?

"The justice of a master or a father is a different thing from that of a citizen, for a son or slave is property, and there can be no injustice to one's own property." *–Aristotle*

The sin of child abuse is hardly new! Throughout most of history, children were not granted individual rights. As second-class citizens, children have often been subjected to sexual abuse as well as physical and emotional maltreatment. Smaller powerless dependents have not always been valued as highly as voting, income generating, productive adults!

In ancient days, a child was looked upon as the property of his father who could do whatever he wished with him. The Code of Hammurabi, based on early Babylonian law, dating back before 1792 B.C., allowed a man to sell his child in payment of a debt or in exchange for goods. The services of child slaves often included far more than laboring in the fields and cleaning houses! Read Genesis 19:1-10 for an account of how even Lot, Abraham's nephew, offered his own virgin daughters to the men of Sodom as substitutes for the male visitors sent from God *(whom the men wanted to rape)*.

Children were considered to be expendable by many, and child abuse was looked upon as simply part of life. Infanticide of defective or unwanted children was common. In Egyptian and other ancient world civilizations, children were offered as sacrifices to the gods.

Even the democratic Greeks failed to respect the rights of children. Affluent, well-respected men engaged in sexual activities with children. Young boys were prized for their softness and sometimes castrated in the hope that they would maintain that quality. Many Greeks practiced *pederasty*, a custom that advocated sexual relationships between mature and immature males. Legal guidelines regulated this accepted practice that purported to raise dexterous soldiers! At the age of twelve, a young boy could be courted by an adult male suitor. When the boy's father approved of the suitor, the man became responsible for the boy's training in all areas of life. Gifts of military equipment were often presented to the youths by the adult male, along with training in the martial arts. The gratification of the educator's sexual desires was expected in return. It was considered an honor to receive the special privileges of an adult lover! This "noble" practice opened the door to forced sexual slavery of boys considered undesirable for army service.[4]

During the time of Christ, Roman mothers left unwanted babies at the foot of the Lactarian column to die or to be picked up by degenerates who would train them to be prostitutes or beggars.[5] The Romans considered sexual abuse a means of humiliation, and frequently imposed brutal assaults and acts of sexual violence upon enemies, slaves, women, and children. The Roman emperor, Tiberius, was a known pederast who enjoyed swimming with and molesting little boys.

Children of the Middle Ages were often loaned out for "service." Many of these children were violently beaten, and few escaped what would be considered severe abuse in today's world.

In the sixteenth century, the legal age of consent was ten, and children often married at twelve. Marriages were usually arranged by a child's parents for convenience or economic gain. Thus, young girls often became brides to men old enough to be their fathers or even grandfathers! This practice has not been limited to the sixteenth century. It still exists in some parts of the world today.

Private bedrooms did not come into vogue until the eighteenth century. Sexual exploitation of children sleeping alongside adults was common. As late as 1832, children were considered victims of rape only when they were younger than ten.

The lot of children in the seventeenth and eighteenth centuries was no better. In England, great numbers of starving children were sent to workhouses where only the strongest survived. Even the children of the royal family were flogged regularly *(unless they were fortunate enough to have a whipping boy)*.

The production and distribution of child pornography and child prostitution flourished during the nineteenth century. Sex merchants found easy prey from the flood of immigrants coming to the New World. An estimated 2,000 little girls who arrived in New York disappeared annually during the middle of the nineteenth century.[6]

Although physical and emotional maltreatment of children was openly practiced in most cultures, child sexual abuse has generally been a forbidden taboo by most of the population. Even so, sexual exploitation has been condoned in a world that failed to ask questions about the rights of children.

At the turn of this century, many welcomed Sigmund Freud's theories about the sexuality of children, for they affirmed the notion that reports of child sexual abuse were nothing to be alarmed about. Although Freud presented a theory in 1896 that attributed the hysterics of many of his female patients to sexual seduction by their fathers, he later retracted the idea. It was apparently too difficult for him to accept his own findings — that his patients had been abused by their supposedly morally-upstanding fathers! He replaced this theory with the idea that children were aware of their feelings of sexuality from infancy, and that reports of child sexual victimization were often childhood fantasies.

Additionally, Freud formulated the Oedipus Rex complex theory. This theory hypothesizes that children sexually desire the opposite sex parent and feel hostility toward the same sex parent. Thus, he concluded, girls wishing to be seduced by their fathers and boys by their mothers "ask for" sexual relations through seductive behavior.[7]

In recent years, some researchers have raised serious questions about the validity of Freud's research which was based primarily on self-analysis.[8] The 1985 publication of deeply personal letters Freud wrote to his close friend, Wilhelm Fleiss, revealed that Freud suffered from a variety of neuroses during the years when he was formulating his major theories about child sexuality. In his correspondence, Freud confessed to a number of anxieties, fears, hatreds, and sexual frustrations as well as occasional use of heavy doses of cocaine to relieve his "migraine headaches."[9]

Unfortunately, Freud's ideas have had a major impact upon society for many years. His theories about childhood sexual fantasies and seductive behavior exhibited by children provided a convenient excuse for society's suppression and concealment of child sexual exploitation. They significantly contributed to the mistaken notion that children who report intrafamilial sexual abuse are frequently lying, or have "asked for" sexual abuse through seductive behavior.

There are organizations in the world today that promote sex between adults and children. The René-Guyon Society lobbied in California for their "civil right" to choose to engage in sex with minors! Promising that sex at an early age will reduce divorce and delinquency, their motto is: "Sex by eight or else it's too late." Other such groups are the North American Man/Boy Love Association and Childhood Sensuality Circle. The Pedophile Information Exchange and Pedophile Action for Liberation are based in England. Others exist in Switzerland, Germany and probably most other countries.[10]

Public Outrage Over Child Abuse *IS* a Twentieth Century Phenomenon!

There have always been compassionate individuals who have tried to put an end to child abuse. But their attempts never made much of an impact on the problem before the late nineteenth century. During the post-Civil War period, times were especially bad, and many babies were abandoned. An order of nuns known as the Sisters of Charity opened a house to receive unwanted infants in New York City in 1869. This was the beginning of the New York Foundling Hospital. In its first year of operation, the hospital received over one thousand babies.[11]

In 1874 one well-publicized case of child abuse proved to be a turning point in the lack of public response to the problem. It involved a nine-year-old girl named Mary Ellen. She had been chained to her bed by foster parents in a crowded section of New York City. She suffered malnutrition and showed signs of having been beaten for a number of years. Concerned neighbors reported their suspicions to a nurse who lived in the area. When the nurse contacted the police and district attorney, they found that there was no legal way to remove Mary Ellen from the home. She was considered to be the property of the foster parents.

In desperation, the nurse and some church workers presented Mary Ellen's case to the Society for the Prevention of Cruelty to Animals. They pointed out that as a member of the animal kingdom she was entitled to their help. Ironically, this organization had the power to remove mistreated animals from abusers. The SPCA filed charges on Mary Ellen's behalf, and the court ordered that she be taken away from the foster parents.

Many were shocked to realize that more protection was available for mistreated animals than for mistreated children. The Society for the Prevention of Cruelty to Children was founded in 1875 in New York. In 1877 the American Humane Association was established with the primary goal of preventing cruelty, especially to children. By the year 1900 there were 161 similar groups in the United States. The organizations reached only those children who had been severely physically abused. They usually dealt with the problem by removing the children from their homes, rather than trying to work with parents and children to improve their family relationships.[12]

Progress continued during the first half of the twentieth century, but the institutions and foster homes that provided care for abused children were not usually adequate solutions. A parent's right to discipline and control his family remained an excuse for much child abuse.

It wasn't until 1961 that Dr. Henry Kempe of the Colorado General Hospital suggested the term "battered child syndrome" for serious physical injuries that did not appear to be accidental.

In 1968 thousands upon thousands of uninformed doctors and parents read **The Battered Child**, co-authored by Dr. Kempe and Dr. Ray Helfer.[13] The impact of the book was tremendous. Citizens called for laws that would protect abused children from further abuse.

By 1970 all fifty states had enacted legislation to specifically identify the problem of child abuse. Legal definitions, penalties for offenses, and reporting statutes were included in the new laws. The National Committee for Prevention of Child Abuse (NCPCA) was established in 1972 to coordinate efforts and develop new ones for child abuse prevention. These and several other country-wide organizations devote full-time efforts to child abuse and neglect. *(A list of organizations is included in the appendix. Consult your local phone book for others that are in your area.)*

In 1974 Congress passed the Child Abuse Prevention and Treatment Act which established a set of uniform operating standards with respect to the identification and management of child abuse cases. The Act also established the National Center on Child Abuse and Neglect within the Department of Health, Education, and Welfare. The center administers federally funded projects, conducts research, collects, analyzes and disseminates information, and provides assistance to states and communities for activities on the prevention, identification and treatment of child abuse and neglect.

The definitions of maltreatment, investigative procedures, policies, and service systems were left to individual states. During the seventies and early eighties, state legislatures enacted numerous laws to try to effectively address the complex problem of child abuse. Consequently there is some variance in state laws, policies, and procedures. One disadvantage of state autonomy is inconsistent reporting and resource information as well as the possibility that a perpetrator might escape prosecution by leaving the state.

During the past two decades, extensive research has been conducted to try to identify the causes and effects of child abuse. Many treatment and prevention programs were initiated. Task Forces have been organized to raise community awareness and response at the local level, and to coordinate and promote a multidisciplinary approach to deal with the problem. Hospitals, educational institutions and many other agencies have focused on efforts to identify, treat, and prevent child abuse and neglect more effectively. The public conscience has finally been shaken from its stupor!

Incidence

In most states, reports of child abuse are categorized into physical abuse, sexual abuse, emotional maltreatment and neglect. Reports of maltreatment of 700,000 children were made in the U.S. in 1976. That figure escalated rapidly to 2 million in 1985 and nearly 2.7 million by 1991.[14,15]

According to records compiled by the American Humane Society, only slightly over 1% of total reports in 1976 were for sexual abuse (7,559). By 1983, child sexual abuse represented 4% of the total cases reported, then 6% of the 2 million cases reported in 1985.

Long believed to be extremely rare, or a problem occurring only in primitive cultures or lower classes, child sexual abuse is now recognized as far more prevalent than once imagined.

Charges in 1984 that up to 125 children in Manhattan Beach, California, were raped, sodomized, and otherwise molested at the respected McMartin Preschool was a catalyst for a domino effect of disclosures of sexual abuse. Examples of the once little discussed crime surfaced everywhere. The McMartin case was finally dismissed in 1989 after a 2½ year trial and $14 million cost to taxpayers.[16] The case alarmed many parents and instilled a widespread phobia about daycare centers. In actual fact, abuse by day care or foster care workers represents only 1% of all reported cases of sexual abuse.[17] Most cases involve victims who were abused by someone they knew well and trusted, many times within their own family.

By 1986, sexual abuse represented 16% of all cases reported, and has remained at approximately that rate through 1991. Reports for the other forms of abuse are as follows: physical abuse – 26%, emotional maltreatment – 8%, neglect – 55%, and unspecified abuse – 8%.[18]

The table below summarizes the growth of the epidemic of child abuse during the seventies, eighties, and nineties:

Year	Total Estimated Reports	Sexual Abuse Reports	Percentage[19]
1976	700,000	7,559	1%
1983	1,477,000	71,961	4%
1985	2,000,000	120,000	6%
1986	2,086,000	314,000	15%
1989	2,407,000	384,000	16%
1990	2,537,000	405,920	16%
1991	2,694,000	441,040	16%

Researchers agree that the actual incidence of child maltreatment is far greater than the number of reported cases.

The National Committee for the Prevention of Child Abuse (NCPCA) reports that 1383 child deaths in 1991 were confirmed as a result of child maltreatment.[20] The actual figure may be as many as 5,000 according to Dr. Vincent Fontana.[21] Some percentage of accidental deaths, child homicides and Sudden Infant Death Syndrome cases might be more appropriately labeled child maltreatment if comprehensive investigations were routinely conducted.[22]

Implications and trends:

1. From 1985-1992 reports increased by 40%, with a steady growth of about 6% each year. This growth rate, while representing a sizable expansion in the number of reports is about half the growth rate from 1980-1985. (11.4%).

2. There was a larger rate of growth of reports between 1990-91. Based on surveys from individual states, the NCPCA attributes this growth to (1) increased economic stress due to poverty, unemployment and related work concerns, (2) increased public awareness, and (3) substance abuse.[23]

3. Of the reported cases, only 40% are "substantiated." That does not mean that 60% are "unfounded." Rather, it means that there was insufficient credible evidence to open a case. The implication is that concerned adults should continue to inform authorities when they suspect child maltreatment even if a case was dismissed after an earlier report. Multiple reports help authorities establish proof.[24]

4. At least half of the unsubstantiated cases are for children who are involved in divorced parents' custody battles. Unfortunately, allegations of child abuse are often wrongfully charged in a parent's attempt to gain custody.[25]

5. Of the fatalities attributed to child maltreatment, 79% of the victims were under the age of five, and 54% were under one year old. Thus very young children are at the highest risk for loss of life due to maltreatment. Prevention efforts should be focused toward parents of young children, particularly those parents known to CPS agencies.[26]

6. A growing number of infants have been born with exposure to illegal substances taken by their mothers during pregnancy. Estimates vary from 100,000 to 350,000 infants nationwide.[27]

7. The child welfare system has become overloaded with cases. This does not mean citizens should stop making reports. However, private crisis nurseries and various family and children's services operated by private organizations are more needed than ever.

Additionally, consider the following estimates based on reported cases and information obtained from studies of sexual offenders, adults victimized as children, and random population samples:

- Numerous studies have found that one out of four girls is sexually molested by age 16. Some studies indicate a higher percentage — 1 out of 3.

- Although boys do not report abuse as frequently as girls, most researchers believe that boys are at equal risk of abuse.
- Eighty-five percent of the abusers are individuals who are known and trusted by their victims.
- Fifty percent of the incidents occur in the victim's or offender's home.
- Incest occurs in one out of ten families.
- Forty-four of the reported cases in one study occurred while the abuser was under the influence of drugs or alcohol.

The heart-wrenching truth is that many, many children are abused sexually in some form by someone they know. The high estimates are substantiated by the fact that most adults can relate a personal incident that happened to them or someone close to them during their childhood. Estimated reports don't include the hundreds of thousands of children who are victims of child prostitution and pornography.

Dr. Nicolas Groth, one of the foremost experts on child sexual abuse who has done extensive work with offenders, calls child sexual abuse an epidemic.[28] In the past decade, many truly have become alarmed at the epidemic, and some feel the nation has reached a point of hysteria over the problem.

It is uncertain whether there is *more* or *less* abuse now than there has been throughout history. Some believe the problem only seems more prevalent because it is more openly discussed. Others contend that the deterioration of family structure and values, along with the unlimited boundaries of sexuality in today's society, have contributed to an increased incidence of child abuse and domestic violence. As mentioned earlier, charges of child abuse frequently accompany custody battles between divorced parents and the increased rate of divorce is a reality. Although at least half of these are unsubstantiated, it is true that there is a greater likelihood of abuse from stepparents than from birth parents. Also, there is increased drug usage, and a high correlation between substance abuse and child abuse has been established.[29] Furthermore, more adolescents than ever before are becoming single parents, and statistics show that young single parents are more likely to maltreat their children. Additionally, the increased acceptance of violence in our society and increasing poverty levels no doubt contribute to the rise in the number of reports.

The three billion dollar child pornography business could also be a major reason for the increase in child abuse. Some parents cite that a general acceptance of the "me first" attitude of personal gratification above all else provides a convenient rationalization for child sexual exploitation.

What *is* certain is that child abuse will never be totally prevented as long as there is sin in the world. That is why instruction about sexuality, personal body safety, parenting education, skills for developing good interpersonal relationships, and God's unconditional love is so important for children and parents!

CHAPTER FOUR

What Type of Individual Molests Children?

"Most of us believe that a child molester will be recognizable as a 'bad' person. We want to believe that the offender will look as horrible as the deed!" –*Flora Calao, Codirector of SAFE*[30]

A number of misconceptions have evolved over the years regarding sexual offenders. The media has helped to dispel many of these myths, but the primary ones warrant repetition.

MYTH #1: **Sexual offenders are weird-looking, demented strangers whose evil intentions are apparent from their appearance!**

FACT: No one really wants to believe that anyone her/his

child knows would sexually abuse her/him. Thus, there has been a tendency to create the illusion that sexual offenders can be recognized by the dirty trench coats they wear, their beady eyes, and the bag of candy they're holding. The truth is that sexual offenders come from all walks of life and all socioeconomic levels. They often appear to be normally functioning members of society, who may be well respected in the community. Some molesters are active church workers! Moreover, in the vast majority of cases, sexual offenders are known and trusted by their victims.

MYTH #2: **Child molesters are "dirty old men."**

FACT: Although some child molesters may very well fit this description, most offenders begin abusing children while they themselves are quite young. Eighty percent of the offenders involved in one study committed their first offense before the age of thirty. In fact, many offenders admit to having abused younger children while they were only teenagers themselves. A study by Vincent DeFrancis showed that the average offender's age was thirty-one. Only 10% of the offenders studied were over fifty, while 20% of offenders were under the age of twenty.[31] However, adolescent sex offenses are significantly underreported and more widespread than officially acknowledged. *(Those who learn about adolescent offenders often mistakenly write off the incidents to "experimentation," and they fail to provide correction and counseling so desperately needed by these young people.)*

Additionally, not all molesters are male. Although the majority of reports are for male perpetrators, some molesters are female. Young boys do not often report abuse from an adult female for fear they will be labeled a sissy.

MYTH #3: **Sexual abuse is a violent, one-time happening.**

FACT: Sexual molesters usually test a child to see how easily the child may be manipulated. Once trust has been established, they often try nonviolent offenses such as showing the child pornographic magazines or inappropriately touching the child. If the child does not protest, the abuse will usually gradually progress to more intimate sexual interaction. Only rarely are incidents a one-time occurrence.

MYTH: #4: **Children often "ask for it" through seductive behavior.**

FACT: A child is never at fault. The offender may be looking for seductive behavior and encourage the child to behave in the desired manner by offering rewards for such behavior. Even if a child imitates observed seductive behavior it is the adult's responsibility to redirect the child's behavior.

(Read Genesis 19:30-38.) Lot's daughters were probably well beyond puberty to even conceive of having sexual relations with their father. Having lived in the evil city of Sodom, they had certainly observed seductive behavior by women in the city. Still, Lot was to blame for allowing himself to become drunk, then engaging in sex with his daughters.

• • • • •

What Is Known About Offenders?

Dr. Nicolas Groth divides *sexual offenders* into two general types:[32]

(1) *Child molesters* — These offenders use nonviolent means to coax and exert pressure on their victims. Some 90% of offenders are categorized as child molesters.

(2) *Child rapists* — These offenders use violence and

intimidation during the first encounter to force a child to meet their sexual needs.

Dr. Groth subdivides *child molesters* into two primary orientations:

(1) FIXATED: These child molesters follow a persistent pattern from adolescence. They are primarily attracted to young boys, in whom they see a reflection of their own youth. They may go to great lengths to become close to intended victims, and in fact seem to get along well with children. Fixated molesters are also sometimes called *pedophiles* in that they consistently select children rather than adults for their sexual gratification. When a child reaches puberty, the sexual attraction usually ends for this type of molester. *Pederasts* are also generally categorized as fixated offenders. Members of North American Man/Boy Love are usually fixated sexual offenders.

(2) REGRESSED: This type of molester may have married, experienced a sexual relationship with his spouse, and become a parent. Very often regressed offenders fail to ever establish a loving, normal relationship with their spouses. Typically this type of individual feels inadequate and out of control of his/her life, and eventually turns to children to fulfill a need for power and control when adult relationships become conflictual.

Groth's studies have indicated a fairly even distribution of these two types of child molesters.

There is no set profile for a sexual offender. However there are certain characteristics that are common to a number of offenders.

- Perhaps the single most significant factor is that at least 80% of sexual offenders were **sexually abused or exposed to sexual abuse of other family members when they**

were children themselves. The offender's family emerges as a primary part of the problem. **Physical and emotional abuse from their families** was experienced by an overwhelming majority. There was often a persistent inadequacy in the parent/child relationship. Many molesters were exposed to extreme violence within their homes or in their associations with peers. Offenders harbor a great deal of anger often at their father for abusing them, and at their mother for abandoning them.

- Many offenders are **in a state of depression when they abuse children.** They feel inadequate in fulfilling their responsibilities as an adult and find a child safer and less threatening than another adult. Throughout their lives, many child molesters were unable to relate well to their peers.

- Most offenders report that they **committed their first sex offense as a teenager** but, when found out, the offense was dismissed as "experimentation." A large majority of molesters have admitted that the onset of their deviant sexual interest began between ages fourteen and nineteen.[33]

- Offenders are often **responsible for committing numerous sexual crimes and molesting large numbers of children.** Studies have indicated an average of seventy victims per offender. One study cited an average of 100 crimes per offender.[34]

- Most offenders are **not diagnosed as mentally ill or mentally deficient.** Less than 5% of offenders are mentally retarded or psychotic.[35]

- Offenders **may lack knowledge about sexuality and may have never experienced a positive male/female relationship.** Their ideas about sexuality are often very distorted.

- Offenders **often feel victimized themselves by society**

and are starved for affection and sexual gratification.

- Offenders may rationalize their abuse of children in numerous ways, but ultimately **regard the child as an object to meet their need for mastery and power.**

Offenders are usually inadequate individuals with poor impulse control. They cannot tolerate frustration, generally have low self-esteem, and are rather insensitive to the feelings and needs of others. They have often been socially isolated, although they may put up a façade to those with whom they come in contact. Many are loners who actually fear adult sexuality.

The same general kinds of deficiencies are often characteristic among adolescent sexual offenders. Many are loners with poor family ties, poor self-esteem, and have problems managing their aggression. Thus, it is critical that adolescents who show tendencies toward child sexual abuse be provided with immediate and intensive therapeutic treatment and counseling. It is important to note that these characteristics have been observed by psychiatrists who have treated offenders who have admitted to abusing children. Child molesters may be very good at masking their problems to unsuspecting parents and children.

• • • • •

How Does a Child Become Involved in an Exploitative Situation?

In a small percentage of cases, the perpetrator forces a child to engage in sex through intimidation and physical force. There is no emotional attachment to the child, and the child may even become the target of the perpetrator's rage and cruelty. As previously noted, it is far more common for the exploitation to be nonviolent and continuous.

Dr. Suzanne Sgroi, a noted medical authority on child sexual abuse, has identified a predictable pattern of victimization for the latter type of child sexual abuse: *sexual exploitation.*[36]

Engagement phase:

Child sexual abuse is most often premeditated and prolonged. The abuse continues because the perpetrator uses his position of power over the child as leverage. The perpetrator looks for opportunities to be alone with his intended victim, and he may spend a great deal of time laying the groundwork for access to the child. The perpetrator is usually very adept at gaining the child's trust and is often trusted by the child's parents. Eventually, the child is left alone with a trusted adult who has a legitimate power position over her. He may compliment the child by telling her how special or how beautiful she is, or how strong he is. Then the perpetrator misuses his power by engaging the child in sexual activity in a nonthreatening way, i.e. "Listen to this joke." "Let's play a game." "Look at these pictures. I'll bet your body is prettier than this girl's." Rewards may be offered in exchange for sexual favors. The message he gives the child is that sexual activity is not only OK, but fun and pleasant. The perpetrator may use the pretext of sex education as an excuse for his advances. Physical force is not usually employed in this phase, and the offender will often be dissuaded if a child resists. The child often senses that something is wrong, but usually does not have enough of a concept of sexuality to anticipate what the perpetrator is leading up to. A child's natural curiosity about sex may allow her to become easily enticed, especially if she is uninformed about sexuality.

Sexual interaction phase:

Depending on the child's reaction to initial tests, the sexual

51

activity will end or progress. The average length of sexual activity with a child is three years when the abuser is a relative, caretaker or close family friend. Of course abuse may be much shorter or longer depending on the variables of the individual situation. The abuse may begin with inappropriate touch or exposure and progress to intercourse or deviant sexual behavior. The child's cooperation should not be confused with consent.

Secrecy phase:

The perpetrator uses rewards and/or threats to keep the child quiet. He may try to instill guilt in the child by telling her how bad she is, and how upset her parents would be if they found out. Particularly when the abuser is close to the child, he may threaten that breaking the secrecy pact will lead to his imprisonment and the breakup of the family. Young children may be frightened with horrible threats such as "I'll kill your mother if you tell."

In some cases, the abuser may be gentle and nurturing during sexual acts. The child may even like the special attention and affection offered, and therefore be willing to put up with the sexual abuse.

Disclosure phase:

All too often sexual abuse continues for an extended period, and the child suffers in silence. However, some children will eventually disclose that they are being abused, accidentally or purposefully. Accidental disclosure usually results from injury, venereal disease, pregnancy, or discovery by another person. Purposeful disclosure often occurs at adolescence when the child seeks to establish other relationships and may be prohibited from doing so by a possessive perpetrator. In the case of intrafamilial abuse, the child may disclose when a sibling is threatened. Disclosure may also occur if the abuse changes to a more objectionable form or becomes too frequent. Often a child will exhibit behavioral clues that abuse is occurring, hoping that an alert adult will pick up on it. Behavioral indicators will be discussed in Chapter 5.

Suppression phase:
Once disclosure has occurred, there is a strong tendency on the part of both the victim and the family to try to suppress the incident. This is especially true when the perpetrator is a family member or close friend. Many people seem to feel that life will be easier if they just pretend that it never happened. Tremendous pressure is often exerted on the victim to retract the allegations.

• • • • •

How Does an Offender React When Confronted With Knowledge of the Abuse?
Although reactions to confrontation vary, offenders typically deny any wrongdoing. Most do not seem to view their actions as sinful. Those who do don't seem to really care. If an offender admits to the offense, he often tries to minimize it by projecting blame to the child for being "seductive" or to his own spouse for not understanding him.

A common reaction from fathers who sexually abuse their daughters is, "I wanted to be the one to teach her about sex before she learned about it from someone who didn't care for her."

Some offenders attest to a belief in Christ, and may even attribute their behavior to religious convictions. During questioning, one married offender who had sexually abused his daughter was asked, "How could you force your own daughter to have sexual relations with you?"

"Because my wife never wanted to have sex with me," he answered.

The non-Christian interviewer continued, "If you couldn't persuade your wife to have intercourse, why didn't you seek sexual gratification from another woman?"

The offender indignantly replied, "I'm a God-fearing man. To have sex with someone outside my home would be sinful!"

Those offenders who abuse children while under the influence of alcohol or drugs often use the substance as an excuse for their behavior.

If offenders express remorse, it is generally remorse at being caught rather than for committing the offense. They don't usually consider that the abuse could be psychologically damaging to the child victim.

However some offenders do express a desire for help and seem to want to change once they are forced to realize what they did was wrong.

•••••

Can a Sexual Offender Change His Behavior?

Henry Giaretto, Director of the Child Sexual Abuse Treatment Program in San Jose, CA, reports successful rehabilitation in 90% of the offenders treated.[37] A number of other sexual offender treatment programs also report a high success rate for "regressed" offenders. Of course, it is difficult to determine whether or not the offender has committed abuse secretly, or how long he will be able to control his impulses. Successful rehabilitation of rapists and fixated offenders is considerably lower.

Dr. Nicolas Groth says that child molesters can never really be cured, as they will probably always have an impulse to abuse children. However, he feels that, like alcoholics, they can learn to control their impulses, and to manage their lives better so that they do not need to turn to children to exert their power.[38]

Rehabilitation is usually a long and difficult process that requires court-mandated participation. In sexual offender treatment programs, treatment goals for offenders include: acknowledgment of the offense and acceptance of blame; acceptance of responsibility and accountability for his actions, and restitution made to the victim if possible; sensitization of the pattern that led to his offense so that he can detect warning signs in the future; management of his impulses so that he seeks gratification in an appropriate way.

Some law enforcement officers and other involved professionals, as well as many private citizens, insist that sexual offenders should receive lengthy prison sentences. But there is significant evidence that indicates imprisonment alone will not change offenders' behavior, and effective sexual offender treatment programs within penal institutions are rare. Realizing this, a number of judges are opting for a sixty day to one year jail sentence for first time sexual offenders who indicate a desire to change. Upon release from jail, offenders are placed on probation for five years with strictly enforced court orders to participate in a specialized treatment program. Optimally, treatment should begin as soon as the sexual abuse has been disclosed, but this is not always possible. The relationship between the perpetrator and victim, the degree of family support or dysfunction, the degree of danger of a second offense, and a number of other complex factors should be carefully weighed in deciding upon the best course of action.

A combination of individual therapy and group therapy is a widely accepted treatment model for offenders. A group of

offenders can exert pressure on one another to accept responsibility for their crimes. Often offenders who fail to see their
own faults easily recognize the shortcomings of others. With
the help of a therapist, they can eventually learn to focus on
their own problems and work toward changing.

•••••

How Can Christians Help Sexual Offenders?

Christians know that God is willing to forgive all sins,
including the sin of child molesting. It would be wrong to
contend that a person can never change and seek God's will.
Christians involved in working with offenders should start by
emphasizing the seriousness of their sins, then explain God's
promise of forgiveness. Some appropriate Biblical references
follow. Leviticus 18:6 is a direct command from the Lord not
to commit incest. Verses 7–18 list specific cases, including
stepchildren and relatives by marriage. Leviticus 20:11–21
outlines the penalties.

In the New Testament Paul addresses the issue of a church
member who had committed incest. The offender was
expelled from the fellowship of the church (I Corinthians
5:1–5). Evidently the sexual offender in the Corinthian church
repented of his sin, for Paul urges forgiveness in II Corinthians 2:5–8.

Jesus confronted the Samaritan woman at the well with her
sin of living with a man she had not married. He pointed out
that she had already been married five times (John 4:18). He
wanted her to admit her guilt before she could receive forgiveness and "living water." Consider the compassion that
Christ showed to the woman who had been caught committing an act of adultery (John 8:4). In His infinite wisdom, He
knew she had repented in her heart, and thus He told her to go
on her way and sin no more. Bear in mind that many sexual

offenders are adolescents or young adults who may have been child victims only a few years ago. They may never have received counseling. They are doing to another what was done to them.

The Bible does not specifically state that child sexual abuse is wrong other than in the case of relatives (Leviticus 18:6). But a study of the Scriptures reveals that God's plan is for a man and a woman to express their sexuality within a faithful, loving marriage relationship. Any other type of sexual relations perverts God's plan and is wrong! Study references that address the correct use of sexual love include: Genesis 1:27,28,31; 2:24; Proverbs 5:15,18,19; Song of Solomon 7:10; I Corinthians 7; and Ephesians 5:23–25, 31–33. Among the passages that condemn sexual behavior outside marriage are Exodus 20:14; Leviticus 18:6–25; 19:29; Deuteronomy 22:28,29; 23:17; Proverbs 7:25–27; Ezekiel 16; Matthew 19:8,9; Romans 1:26–32; I Corinthians 5:1–5, 9–11; 6:9–20; 7:5; Jude 6,7; and Revelation 17:4–6; 21:8; 22:15.

It is essential that a sexual offender clearly understands what he must do to claim God's promise of forgiveness. In addition to an unconditional admission of guilt, he must also repent of his sin. Counselors should emphasize that true repentance involves more than regret. It also means a complete turnaround from sin and a commitment to seek God's will. He should be willing to make restitution to the victim when this is possible. *(In some cases, the victim is better off to never have to see the perpetrator again.)*

A number of counselors have made the observation that it is unwise for one person to try to work with both the offender and victim individually. It seems to be easier for everyone involved when separate counselors are assigned to the offender and victim. The counselors should communicate regularly, and, perhaps at some point in time, the victim and perpetrator can be brought together. However, a very careful assessment of the victim's readiness must be made before she meets with the offender, and she should not be forced to do so.

Those who counsel offenders must also exercise caution in suggesting that a repentant child molester has been "cured." Long-term counseling is always advised, and the offender should be made aware in no uncertain terms that legal authorities will be immediately notified if he commits another offense. If a molester recognizes his sin, repents, and truly wants to change, he should be willing to actively participate in an extended comprehensive treatment program at one of the specified centers around the country.

CHAPTER FIVE

What About the Victims?

"**The problems of adulthood are nothing more than an outgrowth of the problems of childhood.**" *–Dr. Ray Helfer, Childhood Comes First*

Molesters Look for Easy Prey.
All children are potential victims of sexual abuse! There is no stereotypical victim, just as there is no stereotypical offender. Victims have been as young as two weeks old. Some researchers estimate that ten percent of child sexual abuse victims are under the age of five. Different studies have found the average age of victims to be between eight and twelve years, but adolescents are also very vulnerable. Victims are usually subjected to sexual abuse for an extended time period, ranging from weeks to an entire childhood.

Girls are the subjects of more reports of sexual abuse cases than boys. However in a study conducted by the New York Psychiatric Institute, sexual offenders confessed to committing eight times as many sexual crimes against boys as they did against girls.[39] Experts have hypothesized that boys are far more reluctant to report abuse than girls, fearing a threat to their masculinity or an admission of weakness at having been victimized.

Child molesters usually seek victims who can be controlled easily. They look for children who will respond to their rewards or threats and keep the secrecy pact. Particularly vulnerable children are those who:

- are afraid to say no to adults.
- are especially fearful of punishment.
- are especially fearful of being labeled "bad."
- have unmet needs.
- long for love and affection.
- are physically or mentally handicapped.
- are left alone for long periods of time or have limited supervision.
- are not knowledgeable about sex.

Unfortunately, well-behaved, obedient, respectful children are often easy prey for molesters. Many "good" children have been taught never to "talk back" to an adult, to be humble, never to make a fuss, and not to insist on having their own way.

Assertive Children Are Less Vulnerable to Abuse Than Docile Children.

Christian parents need to be careful not to oversimplify the Bible's teachings on obedience and respect for authority.

Following lessons about obedience and respect for their elders, children should also be taught that adults are not always right. They need to understand that courage and boldness are called for when authority is misused. Biblical examples of heroes who demonstrated moral courage in the face of misused authority include Peter (Acts 4:1–22), Daniel (Daniel 6), and Esther (Esther 3:12–8:17).

Children will not automatically know when it is OK to be disobedient. Inexperienced children need practice in *being assertive*. Parents should discuss hypothetical situations in which children should refuse to cooperate if an adult asks them to steal, lie, or do something else they know to be wrong. Specific examples of sexual abuse should be included so children understand that such exploitive sexual behaviors as being asked to look at pornographic magazines, being told lewd stories or jokes, and being touched sexually call for disobedience! Children should know that this permission for disobedience applies to *any* adult who asks them to do something wrong, including relatives, teachers, and babysitters!

Children will feel more confident in being assertive if confronted with sexual abuse when they have been given "rights" over their bodies and feelings. This includes a right to privacy at home, and the right to say no to any touches they do not like, even affectionate kisses from a doting aunt or uncle!

God's promise of rewarding those who follow Him must never be misconstrued to mean that "good" children are always rewarded, and "bad" children will be punished while living on earth. Along with promises that "good" things happen to those who are good, parents need to explain the sad facts of life! *Sometimes "bad" things happen to "good" people that are totally out of their control.* If children clearly understand this basic concept, they will not be so quick to conclude that the abuse occurred because they were bad.

Child psychologists and educators emphasize that children who have been trained to be assertive are not only less likely to become victims of sexual abuse, but they are also less likely to succumb to peer pressure to abuse alcohol and drugs. In fact, assertive children are more likely to stand firm against all sorts of temptations and human injustices.

Why Don't Victims Tell About the Abuse?

Now that child sexual abuse is more openly discussed, many adults are greatly relieved to finally feel free to reveal incidents of abuse from their childhood. For many years, they have been haunted by the burden of their secret. Why did they keep silent?

One Christian woman's story illustrates several reasons why many children do not tell about sexual abuse.

A retired widower had befriended her at the age of twelve. The kind neighbor encouraged her to visit him after school each day. He was always eager to hear what had happened during the day and he provided soft drinks and chocolate bars in exchange for her company. At Christmas he gave her a beautiful dress. The young girl enjoyed the attention and special treatment she received from her friend. Her unsuspecting Christian parents knew the man was lonely and they were glad that their daughter was kind enough to offer him some companionship.

On one occasion, the man told the girl an off-color joke. She didn't understand the punchline, but she laughed anyway when her friend guffawed. The girl was surprised that her friend had told her such a joke but continued to visit him nevertheless.

As time progressed he began to tell her about another young girl of whom he was very fond. He very subtly tried to entrap the girl by making her envious of his affection for the other child. Eventually he told her that he had had sexual intercourse with the other little girl. The girl knew very well that sexual intimacy with a child was wrong and was shocked at the revelation. Still she enjoyed the freedom and special treatment she received at the neighbor's home. She continued to visit him, never even considering that she herself could be in danger.

Little by little, the man engaged the child into conversations about sex, capitalizing on her natural curiosity about sexuality. Looking back the woman was amazed at the length of time the man spent establishing her trust and testing her reactions.

Finally the inevitable happened. He wanted to play a game in which she was to take a pillow off his lap to find a surprise. At this point the girl knew what the surprise would be. Confused by feelings of guilt and curiosity at the same time, she reluctantly lifted the pillow. The sight of the neighbor's penis was too much. "You are a bad man, and I don't ever want to see you again!" she exclaimed. She slammed the door as she left to emphasize her anger.

Luckily she had been assertive enough to put an end to the dangerous game. She remembers feeling insulted and disgusted. Yet when she went home, she said nothing. Days passed. She would see the neighbor walking along the street and feel repulsed, but she never told anyone. The neighbor had never threatened the girl, and she does not remember feeling afraid of him. She knew what he had done was wrong. Her parents were usually supportive, and would probably have believed her but she never told them about it. She vaguely recalls mentioning to her mother that she didn't want to go to the neighbor's house again. Why then, would an assertive, Christian girl with loving parents keep silent about what had happened?

"I felt that I was to blame for the neighbor's sexual advances," explained the woman. "I was afraid my parents would think I was bad for continuing to go to his house after the first time he told me a dirty joke. I had let it go too far because of my curiosity about sexuality. He had trapped me into the secrecy pact effortlessly, simply because I was a "good" girl and "good" girls just don't get involved in such things! I carried the guilt with me for a long time, until I finally asked for Jesus' forgiveness. After that I no longer felt guilty, but I still didn't speak up about it.

"I also felt compassion for the neighbor," she continued. "He truly had been kind to me, and I didn't want to get him into trouble."

The reasons for the girl's silence are common feelings for victims who are sexually exploited by a known and trusted individual. They are:

(1) The victim feels he is to blame for the abuse.

(2) The victim fears that her parents will think she is "bad."

(3) The victim does not want to cause trouble for the offender.

Perhaps when the girl told her mother that she didn't want to go back to the neighbor's house, she was providing a clue. However, her mother may have been busy at the time and dismissed it, thinking her child had simply lost interest in visiting the elderly man.

Other reasons for silence:

(4) The victim may be physically, financially, or emotionally dependent on the abuser.

(5) The victim may be terrified of what the molester will

do if he tells.

(6) The victim may have been doing something he shouldn't have been doing when the abuse happened, and fears he will be punished. *(For example, a child disobeyed his parents' warning not to go to the park alone; then was abused while in the park).*

(7) The victim may fear that he will not be believed. He may even try to tell in veiled terms, then give up if adults do not question him further.

(8) When abuse is particularly traumatic, the victim may block it out of his mind.

(9) The victim may not know the proper words for expressing what happened and adults don't pick up on it.

(10) In the case of intrafamilial abuse, the victim may fear that her family will break up if she tells.

• • • • •

Parents and Child Workers Need to Be Alert to the Physical and Behavioral Indicators of Child Sexual Abuse.

The Christian woman's story demonstrates the fact that even assertive youngsters reared by loving, supportive parents may not reveal that they have been sexually abused. One can never be certain that a child will tell, even when he has been trained in personal body safety. In order to be able to detect sexual abuse, parents and those who work with children should be aware of the kinds of signs that indicate sexual abuse may have occurred.

In most cases, sexual abuse of children is nonviolent. If the abuse culminates in intercourse, penetration is usually non-forced. Thus few victims show physical evidence.

When present, the following *physical indicators* strongly

65

suggest that sexual abuse has occurred:
- bruises or bleeding in external genitalia, vagina, or anal regions,
- swollen or reddened cervix, vulva, or perineum,
- semen around genitals,
- venereal disease in young children.

The following *physical symptoms* indicate that sexual abuse has possibly, but not necessarily, occurred:
- pain, itching, bleeding, or spotting in vaginal areas,
- venereal disease in older children,
- pregnancy,
- broken hymen,
- hematomas,
- lacerations in genital area,
- difficulty in urinating,
- vaginal or penile discharge,
- vaginal infection in young children.

More often children who have been sexually abused will exhibit behavioral indicators of sexual abuse. Most of these could also be attributed to other causes. Thus it is important not to jump to a hasty conclusion without weighing all the factors that affect a child's behavior. These indicators may serve to corroborate other indicators and provide clues requiring further examination.

Possible *behavioral indicators* of child sexual abuse:
- abrupt behavior changes,
- escalating fears and phobias,
- nightmares,
- reluctance to be around an adult that was previously liked,
- irritability, crankiness, moodiness,

- depression,
- self-destructive behavior,
- changes in school behavior or schoolwork,
- poor self-image,
- increased knowledge or interest in sexual behavior,
- inappropriate expressions of affection that are uncharacteristic for the child, such as promiscuity or imitated seductive behavior,
- increased masturbation or exhibiting of open sexual behavior especially in young children,
- intense fear of being left alone,
- extreme behavior pattern of withdrawal or acting out,
- delinquency or aggression, extreme outbursts of anger and hostility,
- pseudomature behavior, façade of sophistication and maturity,
- regression to infantile behavior *(thumb-sucking, bedwetting, excessive crying)*, sometimes even giving an impression of mental retardation,
- poor relationships with peers or total withdrawal from friends,
- withdrawal to a fantasy world,
- alcohol or drug abuse,
- running away,
- threats of suicide,
- refusal to participate in physical activities such as gym or sports,
- abnormal clinging to a parent or trusted adult,
- hints dropped without actually disclosing abuse.

Indicators of *incest* in addition to those behaviors listed above may be:

- role reversal between mother and daughter *(victim may*

have heavy housekeeping or child care responsibilities),

- indirect allusions to a special friend *("I'm afraid to go home," or "I'd like to come stay with you."),*
- extreme overprotection by parents or older sibling, or jealousy of the child's contacts with others,
- father's *(or mother's)* consistent refusal to allow child to participate in supervised social events.

It should be noted that a victim may not necessarily behave negatively toward the perpetrator for two very different reasons: She may be afraid of what he will do if the secret is disclosed, so she is careful not to alienate him. Or she may put up with the abuse in exchange for the reward of affection and special treatment and feel a genuine fondness for him.

• • • • •

The Effects of Child Sexual Abuse Vary Greatly.

Few would deny that an act of violent sexual assault on a child will probably traumatize the child for years to come. Children who are victims of rape usually need lengthy treatment and psychotherapy at different periods during their lifetime.

Yet, when they hear of indecent exposure, sexual touching, oral sex, or in fact anything short of intercourse, many parents and even well-trained medical professionals are apt to say with relief, "Thank goodness nothing really happened." They reassure themselves with the notion that children soon forget hurt feelings.

No one really wants to deal with sexual abuse. It is far easier to pretend it didn't happen and hope it will never recur. A common reaction of parents is a refusal to confront the reality of sexual abuse. Even children who have never lied before may be told, "You must have imagined that," especially when the abuser is someone close to the family. Even in cases in which the perpetrator is not close to the family, parents may feel embarrassed and uncomfortable about the whole thing. Or they may fear their child will be further traumatized if forced to talk about it. Thus, they try to sweep the incident under the carpet as quickly as possible. Hopefully, as more parents are made aware of the devastating effects of abuse, more will be willing to take the recommended steps to help child victims.

The effects of sexual abuse on a child vary, depending upon the child's age and personality, the relationship of the offender, the nature, type, duration, frequency, and intensity of the offense, and finally, the response of those close to the victim if he self-discloses.

First, the bad news!

If intercourse did not occur, the child will not become pregnant, will probably not suffer from physical injury, and hopefully will not contract venereal disease. However, the child's boundaries of personal rights have been violated. The child may feel deep shame and confusion. When nothing is done about the offense, the message to the child is that he really isn't very important and that he deserved what happened to him. Add to this emotional scarring the danger that the offender may abuse the child again. If not, the offender will almost certainly molest other children.

The severest effects of sexual abuse include depression, self-destructive behaviors such as alcohol and drug abuse, attempted suicide, self-hate, and an inability to ever regain emotional stability. A high percentage of individuals who suffer from severe psychoses such as multiple personalities were child victims of sexual abuse. A majority of female drug addicts were incestuously abused.

Many victims of abuse continue to function, but suffer from low self-esteem and guilt, and they have difficulty relating to others. Some victims seem to have two separate personalities, one they show the world, the other a hidden depressed state of fear, isolation, and anxiety. A "victim" mentality may emerge in the mind and developing personality of a young child, causing him to be easily victimized repeatedly during his childhood and even as an adult.

Long-term physical effects include colitis, ulcers, venereal disease, migraine headaches, severe backaches, and stomach disorders. A number of adults molested as children describe feeling a "knot in the pit of their stomach" that never goes away or "a lump in the throat" from "holding back a cry."

As adults these victims often become victims of domestic violence and rape. Many seem to lack the general instinct for self-protection. One Chicago study of prostitutes revealed that sixty-nine percent of these women had been introduced to sexuality by their fathers. Promiscuity was the best way they knew to obtain affection.

A large majority of offenders report that they themselves were sexually abused as children. Thus, the uninterrupted cycle often repeats itself. *At least eighty percent of the prisoners in state penal institutions were abused in some way as children.*[40]

If the victim who receives no counseling or support manages to escape the worst effects, he will still probably feel betrayed by a noncaring, nonresponsive society, and he may suffer from a loss of self-worth. The memory frequently interferes with the victim's ability to reach sexual fulfillment and joy as an adult. Sexual pleasure and closeness become associated with the fear or guilt stemming from the childhood abuse.

Sexual abuse is a betrayal of the most fundamental tenet of an adult/child relationship, and the costs are often immeasurable. *But the psychological damage that occurs when a parent refuses to believe or talk with a child can be worse than the incident itself.*

There is some good news!

Victims can recover from even the most severe forms of sexual assault and escape the lifelong effects described above. When victims who disclose that they have been abused are believed and supported, they can view the abuse as a wrong that was committed against them without shouldering the blame.

Victims can be validated through the knowledge that their parents loved them enough to believe them, advocate for them, and act on their behalf. When supported by her own father, a female victim of a male sexual offender will have a more positive attitude toward men than a victim who has no male model she can trust. Victims can emerge with a stronger confidence in their ability to handle difficult situations in life. They can learn how to use community resources to meet their needs, and they will be more likely to seek assistance for problems in the future.

In short, the negative experience can become a catalyst for the development of a greater self-confidence and a more positive outlook on life.

CHAPTER SIX

How Should Adults Respond to a Child Who Has Been Sexually Molested?

"Every child deserves a chance to grow up with a healthy mind and body." *–Dr. James Dobson*[41]

Believe and Support a Child Who Tells You About It!

If a child discloses to you that he has been abused, or if you have observed indicators that lead you to suspect abuse, it is vitally important that you take action immediately. Just by reading this book, you have taken the essential first step toward supporting victims of child sexual abuse. An educated awareness of the problem with all its complexities and implications will help prepare you to deal with it.

Disclosure of child sexual abuse usually causes feelings of rage, alarm, and desperation for parents or other adults who are close to the victim. The desire to write it off to a big mistake is so strong that many adults react with disbelief. *However, children rarely lie about sexual abuse.*

No matter how alarmed or upset you feel, force yourself to keep control of your own emotions as you listen to the child. *(You may need support yourself and you should seek help later when the crisis at hand has passed.)* The child is probably already under stress. He should not be made to feel he is causing problems for the person he has trusted enough to tell. Whatever the circumstances surrounding the incident, do not make the common mistake of placing the blame on the child! The adult offender is *always* responsible for his sinful behavior and his misuse of his position of power over the child.

Listen carefully to what the child says as well as how he says it. As pointed out earlier, children will often drop hints to test an adult's reaction before revealing they have been abused. Young children may sense that someone did something that made them feel uncomfortable, but they may not fully understand that they were abused.

One five-year-old casually asked his mother why Mr. Nolan always laughed when he tickled him. The child's mother smiled, picturing the young man who was always so kind to the children for whom his wife baby-sat. He worked at night and was often available in the afternoons to help entertain the crew of active preschoolers. The mother felt fortunate to have found such a caring couple with whom to leave her children when she went shopping.

"Why honey," she replied, "most people laugh when they tickle someone because they are having fun. Your daddy laughs, too, when he tickles you."

The child still didn't understand so he rephrased his question. "But why does he laugh when he tickles me inside my underpants?" he inquired frowning.

At this, the mother took a quick breath, suddenly compre-hending the impact of what her child was indirectly telling her.

"Can you tell exactly how Mr. Nolan tickled you, Robby? Where did he put his hands?" she asked with calm serious-ness.

Robby lowered his head. "He told me you'd be mad at me if I told you," he answered softly.

"Robby, Mr. Nolan was wrong. I'm not mad at you. In fact, I'm very glad you told me about this. Where did Mr. Nolan touch you, honey?" she repeated gently.

"He put his hand inside my pants and tickled me on my private parts," explained Robby.

After forcing the lump back down her throat, Robby's mother proceeded to ask questions about when and where the incident had happened, who was around and what the child did. She asked the questions matter-of-factly, taking care not to frighten or upset her son. She was relieved to learn that her son had not only left the room immediately, but he had stayed near Mrs. Nolan for the rest of the afternoon.

The mother explained to Robby that Mr. Nolan had done something wrong to him. She reassured him with a hug that she was happy he had told her about it. She spent much time talking with the child about his feelings and providing sup-port for him.

It is most important that a child who discloses abuse is not further traumatized. Assure the child that you believe him and that he did the right thing to tell about the abuse, even if he had been told to keep it a secret. Praise him for his courage and honesty. Tell him that what happened was not his fault and that you will get help for him. Write down what the child has told you. Do NOT ask leading questions or "put words" in the child's mouth.

If the child expresses feelings that disturb you, refrain from criticizing him. It is better for him to "get out" the feelings than to suppress them. Remain supportive and controlled. The child needs to be reassured that touching is usually good. Unless it seems to make him uncomfortable, gently hold his hand or put your arm around him.

Be careful not to make promises that may not come true! If the child is frightened of the perpetrator, indicate that you will get help so that he will be safe from further abuse. If, however the child is very close to the perpetrator and fears that he will be sent to jail, simply tell him that you will see that the perpetrator gets help. Do not verbally attack the perpetrator and do not promise that he will not be arrested.

Experts advise that authorities should be contacted to conduct questioning as soon as suspicion of abuse has been established. Too much interrogation by untrained adults is often more detrimental than helpful.

Finally, do not confront the offender with knowledge of the abuse before a child's safety has been insured.

Incidents of Child Sexual Abuse Should Be Reported to the Appropriate Authorities.

Reporting an incident of sexual abuse is never easy. It is especially hard when the offender is a close friend or family member. Even when the abuser is a stranger, many parents do not want to subject their child to questioning and the legal process. However, making a report of an incident of sexual abuse is necessary for several important reasons:

Though difficult, having a child make a statement to investigators affirms for her that the incident was not her fault.

Reporting serves to protect not only the victim, but all

other children the molester may come in contact with. As previously discussed, child molestation is seldom a one-time offense. The offender may have been abusing children for years, and he will probably continue in this pattern unless there is legal intervention.

The offender needs to be confronted with his crime and held accountable for it. Beyond his need for punishment is his great need for help in order to change his way of life. No one individual should ever assume sole responsibility for trying to rehabilitate a child molester. Rehabilitation usually requires law enforcement, court orders, and extended specialized therapy. Thus, reporting sexual abuse is the first step toward helping a child molester.

Reporting sexual abuse also means that medical care, counseling or other services will be provided for the victim and his family if necessary.

Most states have enacted laws that mandate professionals who come into contact with children to report suspected cases of child abuse. Mandated professions usually include doctors, other health care personnel, social workers, teachers, police officers, lawyers, clergy, therapists, and all individuals working with children in a professional capacity. *Mandated reporters can be held civilly liable for damages if they fail to report a case of child abuse.*

Copies of state laws that define child abuse and the reporting procedure are available from local departments of social services, law enforcement agencies, or district attorneys' offices. Most schools have a specific policy and protocol for reporting child abuse. Even if you are not mandated by law to make a report, conscience should dictate that help is needed for the child.

In general, an official report should be made when:

(1) A child discloses that an adult eighteen or over has had sexual contact with him. Sexual behaviors include intercourse, fondling or touching, anal or oral sex, or taking sexual photographs.

(2) A child was forced or tricked by an adult into having sexual contact with another child.

(3) Another individual states that someone has reported sexual abuse to him. *(Example: A victim's parent tells of abuse but refuses to make a report to police.)*

(4) Physical evidence of sexual abuse is discovered. *Note:* Abuse by children who are at least four years older than the victim should also be reported. Systems for dealing with adolescent offenders are less clearly defined than for adult offenders. Contact your local Department of Social Services or law enforcement agency for instructions.

Every state has at least one statewide agency mandated to receive and investigate reports. Many states have a central registry that receives reports by telephone. A toll-free number is listed in the emergency number section of telephone directories. State hotlines receive reports of child abuse involving perpetrators who are either family members or a person responsible for the child at the time of victimization. After the report is received, the State Registry will contact the local Department of Social Services, who will send a caseworker to make an investigation. In some cases, a police officer will accompany the caseworker. Local police agencies can also take reports of sexual abuse.

Reports of sexual abuse by offenders who are not relatives or have no responsibility for the child should be made to a law enforcement agency. Check with the local Department of Social Services to find out which law enforcement agency in your community is most qualified to handle these cases.

Some law enforcement agencies have established sexual abuse units to conduct investigations of child sexual abuse. State police departments usually have personnel with specialized training for questioning child victims. **Request that a specially trained officer be sent to interview the child.**

According to Federal Public Act 93-247, effective January 31, 1974, each state must "have in effect a state child abuse and neglect law which includes provision for immunity for reporting . . . from prosecution."

Reporters are guaranteed protection from civil and criminal liability when reports are given in good faith (an honest belief that a child is being abused), even if the report proves to be a mistake. No proof or evidence is necessary to make a report and reporters' names are not normally divulged. Reports will even be accepted from anonymous reporters, although it is far more helpful if investigators can interview the reporter.

All too often people who suspect child sexual abuse are afraid of making false accusations or choose to ignore the possibility that it did occur. By failing to make a report, they abandon their duty to the victim, his family, and society. Many localities have Crime Victims Assistance programs that can provide experienced, compassionate advocates to help the child and family through the process.

A Medical Examination Is Generally Advised for Victims of Sexual Abuse.

Very often disclosure of abuse does not occur immediately following the incident. However, if a child discloses that she has been subjected to sexual penetration or oral sex, a medical examination is always advised as soon as possible.

Try to locate a physician who is accustomed to examining sexually abused victims, and who will be sensitive to the child's feelings. If your family doctor is not experienced in working with child victims, seek a specialist. The local Department of Social Services should be able to make a recommendation. Before taking the child to the doctor's office, explain to her what will probably be done and why.

A gentle medical examiner will not only be nonthreatening, but he/she can actually reassure the child who fears she has been harmed. Both the child and her parents should be informed of what will be done during the examination. The child's need for privacy should be respected during the examination by allowing her to remain partially clothed. A parent should insist, if necessary, that the child be medically examined in a sensitive and thorough manner.

Dr. Suzanne Sgroi, a medical physician nationally recognized for her work with sexually victimized children, suggests that a medical examination for victims should include at least the following:

- a genital/rectal inspection,
- gonorrhea cultures from the throat, rectum, urethra, and vagina,
- a check for the presence of sperm,
- a blood test for syphilis and AIDS,
- a check for other physical evidence of trauma (bruises, etc.).

For children under six, a skeletal X-ray is often advised.[42]

The possibility of pregnancy should be considered for girls who have reached puberty or are even approaching puberty. Conception is possible up to six months prior to the onset of menstruation. Although the average age of menarche is twelve, it is not terribly uncommon for a girl to begin menstruating at the age of eight. Professional counseling is generally advised, starting as soon as possible. A discussion about the need for treatment is included in Chapter 7.

What Should Be Done About Other Forms of Abuse?

The reporting procedure for other forms of abuse is the same as for child sexual abuse. Many people hesitate to make reports for physical and emotional abuse or neglect. They fear that public agency involvement will be embarrassing and resented by the parents. Certainly, concerned individuals can try to offer assistance to a family before making a report. Frequently, though, abusive families suffer from so many problems that a variety of kinds of professional assistance is needed. Parents may be too frustrated to accept help on their own. An official report is a call for help for both the child and the family.

In *Love Must Be Tough*, Dr. James Dobson speaks to parents about abuse within their own homes.

"Child abuse cannot be tolerated. Its effect on a developing youngster can be devastating. That's why I recommend loving toughness when one parent observes consistent violence being inflicted on a boy or a girl by the spouse. . . . What one permissive parent may interpret as child abuse may be, in fact good discipline by the other spouse. The ideal approach is for mothers and fathers who disagree on techniques of discipline to discuss the matter with a wise, neutral counselor who can mediate the conflict.

"There are hundreds of thousands of homes today where one parent is aware of injustice and cruelty on the part of the other. . . . Worse yet . . . many mothers knowingly permit their husbands to abuse their daughters sexually. . . .

"Mothers and fathers, if this is going on in your home, you simply must come to the rescue of your child! . . . I urge you to seek professional help today. . . . If all else fails and the

abuse continues, get the child out of the house in which it is occurring. That is loving toughness under fire!

"Finally if you are the abuser, don't wait another day to seek professional consultation. . . . Sure, it will be painful to admit that you have hurt your children, but if you'll act now, there may still be time for your son or daughter to recover and live a normal life during the critical developmental years. You will never regret dealing with this terrible problem before it is too late."[43]

From *Love Must Be Tough* by James C. Dobson, copyright © 1983; used by permission of Word Books, Publisher, Waco, Texas 76796.

CHAPTER SEVEN

What Happens After a Report Has Been Filed?

"No longer can it be said that concern about and responsibility for abused and neglected children is the exclusive province of child protective services. Nor for that matter does it belong exclusively to those in the helping profession who have been assigned a specific role of reporting, investigating, or treating. No, the ownership of the problem of child abuse and neglect and the responsibility for doing something about it belongs to all of us." –*James S. Cameron, Director of the New York State Federation on Child Abuse and Neglect*[44]

A Report Should Be the Catalyst for Expert Help!
An investigation will be made by an appropriate agency to determine whether the child is in immediate danger and

whether or not he has been abused. The investigation should be initiated as soon as possible after the report is made, hopefully within forty-eight hours for cases of sexual abuse. The investigation will probably be conducted by a social service caseworker and/or a police officer depending on the status of the perpetrator. If it is necessary for several individuals to interview the child, ask that they do it together if possible. *Thorough and immediate questioning is important, but the child should not be subjected to any more interviews than absolutely necessary.*

Authorities often will not permit parents to remain with the child during the interview. This policy is based on the fact that sometimes children are more willing to discuss the abuse when interviewed alone. If this is the case, make it clear that the child is not to be frightened or alarmed, and that the interviewer should stop questioning if the child becomes traumatized. In some localities, a special child's advocate may remain with the child to provide support during the interviewing process.

Recently there has been a tremendous push for highly specialized training for investigators. Most of these professionals are sensitive, caring individuals. They are usually skilled in obtaining information from children in a nonthreatening way. However if a caseworker or police officer is not as sensitive as he or she should be, insist upon either an improved attitude or a different investigator.

Depending upon the results of the medical examination, the findings during the investigation, and the victim's family situation, a variety of things can happen. The rights, safety, and well-being of the child should be the first consideration. If the case is indicated *(believed to be true)*, immediate steps should be taken so that the abuse stops and the child's safety is insured. If the child's life or health is threatened, a petition may be filed with the court to order that the child be removed from the home. The perpetrator may be arrested, ordered to attend therapy, or if the evidence is insufficient, dismissed. The investigating agency will try to determine what services are needed and help the family obtain them. If the report is unfounded, charges will be dropped and the report will be expunged. In some cases, investigators can link the family with services even when the case is unfounded.

Ideally, the goals of intervention and treatment are to identify whether or not the child is in danger, to guard the child's immediate safety and protect him from further abuse, to assure the victim and nonoffending family members they are not responsible for the problem, to offer treatment services for the victim and his family, and to provide treatment for the perpetrator in line with the offense and the risk to the child and the community.

It is true that "the system" does not always meet these standards, and it is frequently criticized for its shortcomings. In all fairness, citizens should recognize the inherent difficulties in conducting investigations of child sexual abuse, and they should cooperate with the authorities unless the child's rights or best interests are threatened.

Reports for other forms of child abuse are generally acted upon without involving a law enforcement agency. Exceptions include severe cases of assault and battery. The general goal of the child welfare department is to keep the family together unless children are in serious danger. The caseworker works with a family to develop a plan to help correct the problem, and he assists the family in obtaining needed community services.

If families refuse to cooperate, family court petitions may

be filed, and children may be removed from the home temporarily. Permanent termination of parental rights is rare, occurring only when parents have repeatedly abused children or totally rejected them.

Procedures may vary from state to state, but most child protection agencies will respond in a manner similar to the process in New York, illustrated on the Child Protective Services and Family Court flow chart that follows.[45]

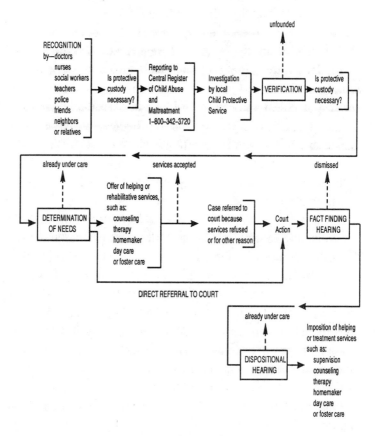

What Can Be Expected During the Legal Process?

So many new laws have been passed in recent years, and so many cases have come before the courts involving child sexual abuse, that it is impossible to make generalized statements that will be applicable in all instances. In general, however, states have passed laws that grant jurisdiction for cases of sexual abuse to two different court systems. One type of law allows district attorneys to decide whether or not to file charges in criminal court. The purpose of the criminal court is to punish the perpetrator.

The other type of statute allows Child Welfare Departments to file cases for presentation in juvenile court or in some states, family court. These courts strive to protect and pursue the victim's safety and interests. Because it has limited jurisdiction over the perpetrator, the family or juvenile court may decide that the only way to insure the child's safety is to remove him from his home if the perpetrator resides there. Sexual abuse cases are often presented in both criminal and family or juvenile courts.

In too many cases, victims have suffered more than offenders during the judicial process. Laws have been enacted in many states to try to minimize the victim's traumatization. Fewer and fewer courts allow evidence to be presented that smears a victim's reputation. The issue is to decide whether or not the allegations that a child was sexually abused are true, not whether or not the child consented to abuse. Most laws now recognize that by definition a child is too young to "consent" to sexual activity with an adult.

Many states have abolished the requirement that a child's testimony be corroborated by a witness, since sexual abuse seldom occurs in front of anyone else! However, prosecuting attorneys often find it difficult to prove that sexual abuse occurred when the child's testimony is the only available evidence. Thus, immediate medical care and interviewing of the victim are important for timely evidence gathering. The greater the time lapse between the incident and the report, the more difficult it is to prove the allegations.

Some localities provide an advocate for the child to help ease the difficult legal process. A child needs a loving, caring adult standing nearby, continually reassuring her that she did the right thing in disclosing the abuse. In addition to providing emotional and psychological support, the advocate can help the child and her family know what to expect in the court process. The advocate should see that the victim visits the courtroom prior to the trial to acquaint her with the surroundings and help relieve anxiety. The advocate can also be a source for ongoing help and follow-up support for the family.

When a case is to be prosecuted in criminal court, the District Attorney should try to keep the time lapse between the original court hearing and the trial as short as possible. Many states give priority to cases involving children. When a perpetrator pleads guilty, the child victim does not usually have to appear in court. Thus every effort should be made to try to convince an offender to admit to his crime.

Perpetrators may be sentenced to imprisonment or jailed for a short term, then released on probation, with a court mandate to attend treatment sessions. Or the case may be dismissed if the evidence is insufficient. One of the most serious problems with criminal prosecution is that a perpetrator who is sent to prison may eventually be released without having received specialized counseling or therapy. *Without ever addressing the nature of his crime, it is unlikely that the offender's behavior will change.*

What Action Should State Legislatures Take?

Many cry in desperation, "What we need are more laws and stiffer punishments for sexual abuse!"

The McMartin case in California precipitated a number of proposed legislative changes designed to make the legal process easier for child victims. For example, more than half of the states now permit a victim's videotaped testimony to be used in the courtroom instead of forcing him to testify in front of the perpetrator. The videotaped testimony allows a child to privately tell what happened right away. The child can only be called to the witness stand if strongly needed.

Many states also use closed circuit television. Via the two-way television, the victim observes the trial, testifies, and is available for cross examination without having to directly face the perpetrator.[47] When live testimony is required, judges should direct attorneys to be especially sensitive in their manner of questioning. They should refuse to allow badgering or intimidation of the victim. In some cases, young children are allowed to testify with a loved one nearby.[48]

At least twenty states have a centralized registry for offenders, available for day care centers and others to use to screen prospective employees.[49] A similar registry has been proposed at the federal level to prevent offenders from crossing state lines to gain employment in child-related fields. TV personality Oprah Winfrey made headlines when she went before Congress to testify as a former victim of abuse for the creation of such a national registry.[50]

Politicians have created quite a maze of proposed legislative changes. But drafting laws to effectively deal with child abuse is easier said than done. Concerned citizens should appeal to local and state experts to help them evaluate the ramifications of proposed legislation before embracing more laws as the answer to the problem. More allocations for establishing treatment and prevention programs need to be budgeted.

Indeed, some judges are calling for more preventive criminal justice measures involving work and treatment programs, especially for adolescents who get into trouble. Since most juvenile delinquents, prostitutes, and violent criminals were abused during childhood, prevention of abuse becomes the best hope in arresting our nation's escalating crime rate. The enactment by numerous states of Family and Children Trust Funds earmarked for abuse prevention programs is certainly a giant step in this direction.

Victims Often Need Ongoing Counseling and Support.

Revelations of adults who were molested as children have contributed greatly to the understanding of the long-term effects on a victim of sexual abuse. Those who were permitted to openly discuss their feelings and who received support and affirmation from loved ones fared best. If no physical violence occurred and the situation is discussed freely, chances are good that a victim may not need professional help and will recover quickly.

In many cases, however, the child may have been sworn to secrecy or threatened with horrendous consequences. The shame, guilt, embarrassment, and fear felt by the child may be paralyzing. To encourage the child to talk about it calls for patience, awareness, and an accepting attitude. Special techniques using puppets, dolls, art materials, games, and toys are often used to help the child tell the story with a minimum of stress. This procedure is best left to experts who have been trained to work with child victims.

It is virtually impossible for a family to deal with a situation of intrafamily sexual abuse without professional help. Families who reason that it is a family problem and must therefore be solved within the family stand little chance of success. The family emotional climate is extremely volatile as members are struggling with different loyalties, confused feelings of love, guilt, anger, responsibility, and so on. The family's existence as a unit is on the line, and the turmoil is too great for them to handle it alone. In all likelihood, the victim will suffer most in a family that refuses to seek outside help.

Many child psychologists recommend that all victims of sexual abuse see a therapist at least once to determine whether or not ongoing counseling is advised. When seeking a therapist, ask about the therapist's training and experience in working with child victims of sexual abuse. If a qualified Christian child counselor is unavailable, look for one who is sensitive to what the child has gone through and is not afraid to deal with it, who seems to put the child at ease, and who will not question his Christian principles. Christian parents are often understandably reluctant to allow a non-Christian to be given a position of influence over their children. In reality, most dedicated child therapists do not seek to undermine a child's religious beliefs, or his respect and love for his parents. Be careful not to allow overprotection to prevent a victim from receiving counseling.

During therapy, the victim should be helped to resolve the experience in his mind and alleviate the trauma. This is often accomplished by encouraging him to express his feelings openly with no judgments imposed. The victim needs to "get it out" and place the responsibility for the crime where it belongs — with the offender. If destructive, acting out, or withdrawal behaviors are manifested, the therapist will try to

There

help the child build his self-esteem and sense of worth to restore him to normal functioning.

Group therapy has proven to be an effective support for victims of sexual abuse. Victims often feel a burning shame and sense that they have been marked as "damaged goods." Just seeing other children who have encountered the same kind of problem is therapeutic in itself. Children will often open up to their peers, expressing feelings that only another victim can fully understand. They learn that others can like them despite what has happened. The group can be the basis for learning to re-establish peer relationships so often sacrificed by victims who have been subjected to continuing sexual abuse. Family therapy may be advised as well, particularly when the abuse was from within the family. The offender must be willing to accept the responsibility for his crime before he can be included in the family treatment.

Don't Forget About the Best "Therapy" Available!

There is no healing power so great as that provided by "The Great Physician." Those who ask for help will certainly receive it. If your child or another child close to you has been sexually molested, claim Jesus' promise to help His followers through steadfast prayer meditation, and Scripture study. *The victim especially needs to be reminded of God's love. One message that probably can't be repeated too often is that God does not blame her or hold her responsible for what happened.* Don't hesitate to seek regular counseling sessions with your minister or another minister outside your community if the child feels uncomfortable with the local minister.

Finally, although counseling and support should be provided for many victims, it is also necessary for them to get on with their lives! Acknowledge their sexual victimization, deal with the realities of the situation, and encourage them to openly discuss their feelings. But *do not dwell on the subject continuously or treat the victim differently from other children.* Victims must be helped to realize that they have much to be grateful for as a child of God, so they can focus on the positive aspects of Christian living.

CHAPTER EIGHT

An Ounce of Prevention . . .

"Every community must take inventory to see whether it has the basic ingredients for a comprehensive, indigenous, and responsible program to meet local needs for the prevention and treatment of child abuse and maltreatment and to aid parents in stress." –*Douglas J. Besharov*[51]

Until just recently, most monies appropriated by governments to deal with the problem of child sexual abuse were used for intervention and treatment programs. Clearly, an after-the-fact, fire-fighting treatment of the problem is inadequate. It would be impossible to effectively treat all the children who suffer from sexual abuse. And the "smoke damage" left after fires have been extinguished can last forever. Somehow, the numbers must stop expanding. Prevention programs and techniques are the only viable answer to the horrendous epidemic of child sexual abuse.

According to Anne Cohn, Executive Director of the National Committee for Prevention of Child Abuse, "The single most promising avenue to preventing sexual abuse at this time is arming children and parents with knowledge about self-protection of children."

Forty-nine states have approved Children and Family Trust Fund Acts to provide budget allocations for wide-scale child abuse and domestic violence prevention programs.

Some state education departments have added child sexual abuse prevention education to their list of required curriculum topics for their schools. Educators recognize the necessity for teaching personal safety skills to school children, and it is tremendously encouraging!

The very best source for this type of instruction though is from well-informed, loving parents. Parents should not wait for the community or the school to assume the responsibility of teaching their child about sexuality and personal body safety. Public lessons may come too late, if at all. Thanks to a heightened awareness about the problem of child sexual abuse, many parents are teaching children about sexuality and personal body safety. Part of this book is a resource to help you do just that from a Christian's perspective.

Inasmuch as You Have Helped One of the Least of These . . . .

"Defend the cause of the weak and fatherless; maintain the rights of the poor and oppressed. Rescue the weak and needy; deliver them from the hand of the wicked" (Psalm 82:3,4, NIV).

Just as many children have never heard about Jesus, many

know nothing about personal body safety skills, or for that matter any safety skills. The fact is that too many parents simply do not purposefully teach their children anything! Christians need to be especially mindful of their duty to protect all children. God loves every child on earth, not just those fortunate enough to have been taught about Him by their parents. **Christians need to take action in their communities to mobilize, support, and expand child abuse prevention efforts.**

Discussions in this book are focused primarily on child sexual abuse. *Yet it is important to realize that a community system for dealing with sexual abuse should be linked with an overall system to effectively intervene, treat and prevent child abuse and neglect in general.*

Child abuse and neglect are caused by a complex set of phenomena. It is not the purpose of this book to go into all the causes and effects. In general, the kinds of emotional scarring caused by sexual abuse are also caused by physical and emotional maltreatment and neglect. Behavioral indicators are numerous, but they are often manifested in the extremes: passivity or withdrawal and aggressive acting out. Although researchers are very hesitant to make definite assertions about the causes and cures of child abuse, the strongest evidence points to four primary inadequacies that are found in a number of individuals who abuse children:

(1) *A lack of sufficient nurturing during childhood.* There is a high correlation between an individual's parental deprivation and her subsequent inadequate parenting. The cycle of abuse is often self-propagating. An abused child learns that family interactions mean violence and verbal attacks, and she will be prone to continue those patterns with her own children.

(2) *Abusive parents usually do not establish a strong initial attachment to their infants.* These parents typically find a baby's cry and other infant demands more annoying than nonabusive parents do.

(3) *Child abusers tend to be more aggressive in their other relationships.* Violence toward children is one manifestation of a general proneness to violence.

(4) *Those who abuse children are less capable of dealing with stress than most individuals. High frustration increases the risk of abuse for those who already have a potential for abuse.*[53]

Abusive and neglectful parents usually feel lonely and are often socially isolated. Major stressful conditions such as an unstable marriage relationship, unemployment, alcohol and drug abuse, excessive demands by children with special needs, legal problems, and overcrowded housing can create a high risk of child abuse. The trigger for abuse may also be caused by less severe stresses for those individuals who have the potential for abuse. Many abusive parents lack parental knowledge and have inappropriate expectations of their children. They often expect children to behave as if they were much older than their age, and they regard their children as capable of adult understanding and response. Very young parents who are still children themselves emotionally often have extreme difficulty parenting. In most cases of parental abuse, the parent becomes frustrated, overreacts to a crisis, and loses control.

The primary focus in treating abusive parents is to "reparent the parent." Goals are to teach good parenting skills through role models and child development and management information, to provide emotional support, and to set limits on abusive behavior.

Since it is impossible to predict which parents will abuse their children, programs targeted at specific populations will not reach all those in need of help. Thus, in addition to primary abuse prevention programs designed to train children in self-assertiveness and personal body safety skills, we need programs that will provide support and parenting education for the population at large.

NO PARENT is totally equipped to deal with all the aspects of child rearing. ALL PARENTS would benefit from readily available information about child development, appropriate discipline, ways for dealing with stress, and other general how-tos to help them meet parenting challenges. Additional services are needed to help alleviate the frustrations of those parents who are "at risk" of abusing their children.

Ideally, a community plan for the prevention of child abuse will include programs to improve parenting at all stages. Listed below are some of the kinds of programs that have been effective. To be successful, abuse prevention programs need the cooperation of all community disciplines and agencies. The multidisciplinary approach is by far the most sensible and efficient way of sharing available resources and services. *Christians can volunteer for community work, adapt programs for parents and children in their own congregations, and join forces with other churches and human service organizations for larger-scale efforts.* (See Chapter 9 for a detailed plan of attack for churches.)

(1) *Prenatal programs* can help prepare parents-to-be for their new roles. Information about child development, ways to communicate with babies, how to handle crying, diaper rash, feeding, and so on can truly make a difference in the

99

way new parents interact with their baby. *Could your church offer a special class for expectant parents?*

(2) *Perinatal bonding*, the psychological attachment that develops soon after childbirth, may be enhanced by allowing unlimited visiting privileges for both parents. Obstetricians and hospital personnel can help *identify* parents who fail to show an early attachment to their babies. These *"at-risk" parents* should be offered appropriate services and education to help them form a more positive relationship with their child. *Does your church provide adequate facilities for infants and new parents, including a clean, well-equipped and staffed nursery and private nursing room? Are meals provided when a mother returns home from the hospital? Do members offer help to new parents?*

(3) *Parent support groups* can be an excellent means for providing parenting education and support. In some communities new parents are paired with skilled parents who can provide support and advice when needed. *Many churches have mothers' groups that meet for Bible study and discussions about topics relevant to their needs. Quality child care is provided so mothers are free to concentrate on interacting with other adults instead of their own children.*

(4) Parents should be encouraged to take their infants to a doctor or clinic for *well-baby checkups.* Some abuse prevention advocates think the *lay health visitor system* used in some European countries could be instituted in the United States. In this system, a caring, supportive individual periodically visits the child and parents at home to check on his health. If this service were routinely provided, frustrated, isolated parents who aren't coping well could receive help without feeling threatened. *Perhaps members of your church could modify this concept with a helping program for new*

parents in your congregation. **Note:** Home visits should be arranged with parents in advance and never be insisted upon. Do not go into homes unwelcomed. The key idea is offered assistance for everyone, not mandated help for potential child abusers!

(5) *Early childhood screening and treatment programs* are necessary to help parents provide adequate care for children with health and developmental problems. *Could someone in your church be appointed to pay special attention to the needs of children in your church who may be physically or mentally handicapped? Bringing handicapped children to church can be a real chore for parents when no provisions are made for their care.*

(6) *Neighborhood walk-in centers* have been established in some communities. These centers offer a large variety of services for parents and their children. They range from counseling services to emergency child care, and they are a veritable oasis for parents who feel overwhelmed. *Could you join another group, a human services organization or another congregation, to staff such a meaningful outreach project in your own neighborhood?*

(7) *Child-care programs* should be available for both working parents and those who need occasional out-of home care for their children. Provisions need to be made for those parents who cannot afford to pay for child care. *Would you like to see your young church membership explode? Offer a part-time, parent-staffed cooperative child-care program for children in your congregation and watch your families grow! This is a tremendous way to help change Sunday-morning acquaintances to everyday friends!*

(8) "Teen Parents," "Parents Anonymous," "Parents United," and other *specialized groups* should be available for

101

parents who express a need for help. These mutual aid groups reduce isolation through the development of peer support systems. *What about parents of teenagers, single parents, and working parents? These folks often need all the support and advice they can get!*

(9) *Adequate crisis services* with well-trained staffs are very important. All too often people take it for granted that these services exist, only to find out in an emergency that they do not. Included in these services are a local crisis hot line, crisis pregnancy centers, and emergency shelter for runaways, battered women, those who are homeless, and those who need medical care. These services often rely on compassionate volunteers from the community. *Does your church provide help to meet crises for members and others who seek it? Could someone in the church serve as a liaison to help link individuals with community services? Could a core of volunteers from your church help staff some of these services in your community?*

(10) *Specialized treatment centers* for abused children are needed to minimize the long-term effects. Some daycare centers for abused children teach abusive parents how to react more positively with their children through role modeling and participation. One agency should be designated to evaluate and coordinate treatment for sexual abuse victims. *What a meaningful way this is to use professional or volunteer skills in providing the loving help so needed by these children and parents!*

(11) *"Education for adulthood" programs* can teach children interpersonal skills and knowledge that will help prepare them for assuming adult responsibilities. *Churches already provide training in Christian principles in Sunday School classes, but they could probably expand instruction about the*

"how-tos" of adult life. Practical training in such topics as personal finances, communication skills, job searching, and time management could be offered during the week. More emphasis could be placed upon techniques and methods for coping with stress, loneliness, depression, handling tempta- tion, developing positive personal relationships, discovering one's talents, and so on. Taught from the perspective of "The One who wrote The Book" these could be wonderful helps.

(12) *Parenting education classes* should be provided on a broad scale. Parenting information is usually available to those who seek it, but "at-risk" parents do not usually attend such classes. Young parents who did not experience a nurtur- ing childhood may not know even the "basics" of child rear- ing. Even those who have studied child development and psy- chology and were brought up in loving homes, may have difficulties adapting to the nonstop, often stressful job of attending to a helpless infant! In order to better prepare young adults for parenting, some communities are initiating classes in parenting education in high schools and junior colleges. *Could your church add Christian parenting classes to high school and young adult programs? Could Christian parenting classes be provided for adults? Rather than being left alone in the nursery to baby-sit, could teens serve as assistants to experienced parents in programs for babies and youngsters? This training would help them learn how to interact positively with children.*

(13) *Educational programs for the community at large as well as specialized trainings for professionals* should be ongoing. The concern about child abuse should not be allowed to fade away. *Are there good public speakers, writ- ers, or professional child workers in your church who could become actively involved in community training?*

Numerous primary prevention programs are in operation in many different parts of the country. Specific information about those programs can be obtained from the National Committee for Prevention of Child Abuse. *(See address in the appendix.)*

CHAPTER NINE

The Role of the Church
In Combatting Child Abuse

"Let the little children come to me, and do not hinder them, for the kingdom of God belongs to such as these."
–*Mark 10:14*

Although many individuals and organizations have been battling child abuse and neglect since the mid-1970's, churches have been reluctant to become involved. Recently, however, many Christians have become aware of victims within the church and realize that child abuse can occur in any neighborhood or congregation.

Indeed, some churches have been sued for "negligent hiring" or "negligent supervision" as a result of sexual molestation of minors by church workers. Unfortunately, churches sometimes attract child molesters because they provide immediate and direct access to children in a trusting and often unsupervised environment. Numerous churches have been plagued with cases of abuse within the congregation. Most have been ill equipped to properly deal with individual cases. Much damage has been suffered, not only by child victims and their families, but also by church leaders and entire congregations.

Thankfully, many churches are becoming proactive with regard to child abuse. A number of churches have initiated actions to provide help for victims and dysfunctional families, and have developed policies and programs geared toward the prevention of child abuse and neglect.

What can Christian churches do to effectively respond to victims of child abuse and neglect?

Church leaders should:

   1. Educate themselves about child abuse.

   2. Develop a comprehensive plan for addressing the problem, starting with a clear policy of how to deal with child abuse cases within the congregation.

   3. Arrange special training sessions about child abuse.

   4. Seek specialized counselors to work with victims and abusers.

   5. Initiate or participate in primary abuse prevention programs in both the church and the community.

A comprehensive step-by-step approach follows:

I. Consult With Church Leaders and Plan an Abuse Prevention Program

The staff and board should meet with a qualified child

abuse consultant to discuss the need for a child abuse prevention program. Your local child welfare agency may be able to suggest a consultant. Work with the specialist to develop a customized plan of action that will be feasible to implement in your church programming. If no specialist is available, a medical professional, teacher, or other concerned church member may volunteer to locate the needed resources for developing your program.

Identify one individual in your congregation who will accept responsibility for initiating and coordinating the development of the program. If possible, locate several individuals who can serve together as a Task Force to keep the effort rolling. The various components of a comprehensive program are described in this chapter.

II. Become Acquainted With the CPS Supervisor

The supervisor and workers of the Child Protective Services Department (CPS) of your county's social services center should be able to offer suggestions for your trainings, your policies, and any specific problems you may have. The coordinator of your program or one church staff member should visit the CPS office to establish rapport and obtain first-hand information about local procedures. It is advisable for one individual to be the consistent contact with the agency to develop a trusting relationship.

The CPS supervisor can probably tell you which law enforcement agencies have specially trained officers who know how to handle abuse cases sensitively. The supervisor may be willing to offer advice when you are uncertain about how to handle a report. She can also provide feedback about a particular case to the person who reports it. The information flow will be easier when the church representative and the

CPS supervisor are already acquainted.

III. Train Your Staff and Board

Next, educate the staff and board about the dynamics of child abuse and your church's legal responsibilities. Some states mandate child abuse training for paid staff members of any organization that serves children. The coordinator should meet with a few primary leaders to ensure full support, then arrange a one- or two-hour training for your staff and board. The training should include discussions about statistics, the causes, effects, dynamics, and legalities, as well as prevention strategies for child abuse and neglect. Encourage leaders to read this entire guidebook to increase their understanding.

Additional resources may be obtained from the National Committee for Prevention of Child Abuse, based in Chicago. There are NCPCA-affiliated organizations in many counties. These organizations usually provide educational literature, films, and training seminars. Or, your local CPS may be able to suggest a trainer and information about community resources.

Obtain copies of your state's child abuse laws from your CPS Department or the District Attorney's office. Give each person a copy of your state's laws. Ask the trainer to go over the laws so that the staff and board clearly understand what behaviors are and are not considered abusive and neglectful. (See Chapter 2.) Discuss also the signs of abuse, reporting procedures, guidelines for discipline and display of affection, and how to respond to a child who discloses he/she has been abused.

Leaders should be made aware that in addition to their moral obligation to help protect innocent and powerless children, the church staff also has a legal obligation to report suspected cases of abuse and neglect to the proper authorities. Most state laws specifically include the *clergy* in the list of professions mandated to report suspected cases, along with doctors, nurses, teachers, and others who work with children professionally.

Additionally, an individual who is considered a *child custodian*, such as a youth leader or a teacher, might be held liable if a child is abused while under his or her care. Custodians are usually required to make a report when they suspect a child is being abused or neglected. Many states enforce criminal penalties when professionals responsible for children fail to report suspected abuse or neglect.

These measures will make a strong statement and discourage abusive behavior by anyone on your staff.

IV. Develop a Written Policy About Child Abuse

The coordinator and Task Force should then assist the staff and board in developing a written policy to serve as a vehicle for communication about the church's position regarding abuse and neglect. The policy should include:

1) A rational statement, listing local county child abuse and neglect statistics.

2) A summary of the legal definitions of abuse and neglect.

3) The state reporting laws and penalties.

4) The names of members of a child abuse consultation team who is responsible to determine how best to handle any suspected cases within the congregation. (For example, the team might consist of the senior minister, the chairman of the board, a psychologist, a nurse, a social worker, and an individual member specially trained about child abuse. See the example policy on pages 116-122 for further explanation of

the consultation team's function.)

5) An outline of the reporting procedure, including the local Child Protective Services telephone number, and the name of the team member responsible to make the report.

6) Follow-up plan.

7) Staff and volunteer screening guidelines. (Check to see what your state requires of individuals who work with children. Churches are not usually bound by state regulations, but you might consider taking the precautions available in your state. For example, local police or state agencies might be able to check to see if an applicant has a criminal or child abuse record.)

8) Volunteer education plan.

9) Guidelines for appropriate discipline and touching of children by teachers and youth workers.

Ask an attorney to review the policy to make sure it complies with local legal requirements. Then go over it with the church board and staff.

All volunteers who work with children should be asked to read the policy. The fact that the church has given such specific attention to the issue should reduce the likelihood of abuse by anyone working with children in the church. It will also emphasize the high value the congregation places on its children, and will help foster an attitude of respect for children by those who work with them.

(See pages 116-122 for a model set of goals and child abuse policy developed by the Mason Church of Christ in Mason, Ohio.)

V. Screen and Train Teachers and Youth Workers
If you educate your congregation about child abuse and

make it clear that you are doing everything possible to ensure the health and safety of the children, workers will understand why they are being carefully screened, and will probably be glad to comply.

Ask all those who work with children to attend a training on abuse and neglect to learn how to recognize symptoms, how to respond to victims, and what they can do to help prevent it. Give each worker a copy of your policy, and go over it with them. Be clear, but also sensitive to your volunteers' feelings during the training. After all, most workers would never think of harming a child!

Emphasize to workers the importance of helping children build positive self-esteem. A child who is confident about his value in God's eyes is more likely to resist an abuser, a bully, or a temptation to do wrong.

VI. Train Parents About Child Sexual Molestation

Offer a training session for your congregation's parents on "How to Reduce the Risk of Child Sexual Victimization." Stress how important it is for parents to teach their own children about sexuality and personal body safety. Give parents specific information and resources to help them know how to handle this kind of instruction. (See Chapter 10.)

VII. Provide Personal Body Safety Instruction for Children

Children need to know that God loves them and wants them to be safe and cared for. They need to be reassured that most adults do not want to harm them. They should also know how and where to turn for support and help. Christian teachers and youth workers should emphasize their availability to children to help with any problem, and work to build trusting relationships.

Offer classes to teach children about personal body safety and what to do if they find themselves in a situation that could lead to sexual abuse. Churches might offer the course for children and parents to attend together. A separate course might be offered for those children whose parents cannot attend with them, since many parents will not talk about personal body safety at home. Discussions about abuse should be tailored to fit the understanding of different age levels. And parents should be encouraged to provide this instruction at home. Use the course *Good Hugs, Bad Hugs: How Can You Tell?*, along with this guidebook as a basis for the instruction, adding films or other resources available in your community.

VIII. Offer Parenting Education to Parents

Christians have a tremendous advantage in child abuse prevention work! Our model of parenting is based upon the Heavenly Father's loving relationship with His children. The Bible is the best parent resource book ever written! Churches need to apply Biblical principles in creative and nontraditional ways that address the problems facing today's families.

No parent is totally equipped to deal with every aspect of child rearing. All parents would benefit from information about child development, appropriate discipline, building a child's self esteem, interpersonal communications, sex education, dealing with stress, dealing with tough social issues, and other practical know-hows for meeting the challenges of parenting. Include some or all of these topics in elective courses offered in your church's program, utilizing some of the wonderful films, courses, books on parenting, and other available resources. Many churches offer such courses on Sunday or Wednesday evenings.

IX. Offer Family Support Programs

Many churches today offer a variety of family support programs designed to provide help for families, to enrich their relationships, and to foster healthy physical and spiritual development. Bible lessons about relationships and good character building can be applied to family life in the nineties.

Churches could start a class for expectant parents and continue the group after their babies are born. Skilled parents can be paired with new parents to provide personal support.

A number of churches provide some type of preschool program, ranging from full day-care/preschool programs, to part-time programs such as "Mothers' Day Out," to baby-sitting cooperatives to babysitting referral services.

Parent support groups are also popular. Parents of children who are in the same age group get together to discuss issues and concerns they are facing with their children.

Separate groups might be formed for single parents, expectant and new parents, teen parents, and parents of teens. Mutual self-help groups can reassure parents that they are not alone in the problems they face, and allow parents to share solutions that have worked. They reduce isolation and encourage support among people in similar circumstances.

"Secret Service" programs match individuals in the church with other members who can provide a needed service for them free of charge.

Many other programs can be designed to help enhance the quality of family interactions and provide relief for parents under stress.

X. Prepare Young People for Adulthood and Parenting

"Education for adulthood" programs teach children and young adults personal skills and attitudes to prepare them for adult responsibilities. Churches can offer practical training in personal finances, communication, job searching, time management, and other skills. Personal development training might include techniques to develop positive personal relationships, discover one's talents, and handle stress, loneliness, and depression.

Education about sex and human sexuality should be included for all ages, beginning in the later elementary years. Sex is a focus in our society and the world's message is not usually the one we want our children to receive. Churches should emphasize the Christian perspective of human sexuality and God's wonderful plan for sex within marriage. The issues of family violence, AIDS, teen pregnancy, abortion and child abuse should be specifically addressed, as these problems do occur in the homes of Christians!

Young adults and teens should prepare for parenting before they assume that tremendous responsibility. Churches can include parenting education in high school and young adult programs. Teens might serve with experienced parents as assistants in the church nursery or toddler class. Learning from good role models is more beneficial than being left to baby-sit with no training.

Courses such as these should not replace Sunday school, but they could be scheduled at other times in the church's education program. Many churches now offer programs on Sunday night or during the week to meet the needs of families.

XI. Provide Individual and Family Counseling Services

Increasing numbers of congregations are offering specialized counseling services for their members. For example, the Mason Church of Christ provides office space for a pastoral counselor as well as a psychiatrist in private practice. The staff refers individuals and families who need on-going counseling and psychiatric care directly to these specialists. Victims and their families often need help that only a specially trained Christian counselor or psychiatrist can provide.

XII. Become Involved in Community Outreach Programs

There are numerous ways in which churches can become involved in community abuse prevention efforts or activities designed to help abused and neglected children or families and individuals under stress. One example is the growing movement among churches to join together with other community churches and citizens to open local crisis pregnancy centers.

Other ideas include volunteering as a core of workers to staff a crisis telephone line, work in a crisis pregnancy center, or help in a neighborhood walk-in center.

Your church can help agencies that deal with or work to prevent child abuse. Your building might be used for community training seminars, support group meetings, or special programs for children. Perhaps there are loving parents in your congregation who could become foster parents for abused children. Someone in your church could serve as a liaison to link individuals with community services.

Your church can initiate abuse prevention programs as an outreach ministry. Clovernook Christian Church in Cincinnati offers Sexual Molestation Prevention workshops for young people and their parents in their community. Your church might offer the *Good Hugs, Bad Hugs: How Can You Tell?* course or some of the other previously described educational courses to the community. Your church might sponsor a community day-care center or baby-sitting cooperative. (See Chapter 8 for other ideas.)

In addition to supporting community food and clothing drives, many churches "adopt" several families who have little financial support.

GOALS OF THE CHILD ABUSE PREVENTION PROGRAM
Mason Church of Christ, Mason, Ohio

I. To protect the children of our congregation from suffering abuse of any form by a member of the church staff, volunteer workers, or anyone else, including their own family members.

II. To instill a respect for children and promote positive interactions with children between the staff, volunteer child workers, and parents.

III. To teach children about personal body safety so they know what to do about potentially dangerous or abusive situations.

IV. To help prepare children and youth to become warm, loving parents themselves by teaching them some of the basics about child development, positive family interactions, and nurturing parenting attitudes and skills.

V. To provide on-going parenting education and support for families.

Child Abuse Policy
I. Rationale

Child abuse is one of the most serious problems in today's world. It is a problem that multiplies itself. For example, 90% of all violent crimes are committed by people who were abused as children. And victims of abuse are at risk of growing up to become child abusers themselves

---

THE ROLE OF THE CHURCH IN COMBATTING CHILD ABUSE

unless the continuing cycle is broken by outside help. The emotional scars of child abuse often last an entire lifetime.

The scope of the problem is monstrous, with over 2.7 million children being abused in the U.S. annually. In Hamilton County, there were 5314 cases of child abuse and neglect reported in 1990. Of these about 54% were for neglect, 16% for sexual abuse, and 8% for emotional maltreatment. Of course, many more cases were never reported.

We must all work to solve the problem, for the sake of our children, our families and our society. We have both a moral and civic duty to help prevent child abuse and to intervene for powerless child victims. Ohio law requires that anyone with knowledge about child abuse report it to the proper authorities.

This policy outlines the steps that should be taken when anyone in our congregation suspects a child is being abused.

II. Ohio Law Regarding Child Abuse
A. Definitions

(Highlights of The Ohio Revised Code, Sections 2151.03, .04, .05, and 2919.22)

Child abuse is nonaccidental, serious harm to a child under eighteen by an adult responsible for the child. The harm can be physical, sexual, or emotional. Physical abuse involves nonaccidental injury. Sexual abuse is committing any act of a sexual nature upon a child, or the allowing of a sexual act, including pornography or prostitution. Emotional abuse is a chronic attitude, pattern of behavior, or acts that interfere with a child's psychological or social development.

Neglect is the failure to act on behalf of a child. Physical neglect is the failure to meet the requirements basic to a child's physical development, such as supervision, housing, clothing, medical attention, nutrition, support and education. Emotional neglect is the failure to provide sufficient affection, support and nurturing necessary to a child's healthy psychological and social development. Neglect may result in the failure to thrive condition marked by retardation or cessation of growth.[1]

B. Reporting Laws
   (Highlights of The Ohio Revised Code, Section 2151.421, (A) (1))
   Everyone **should** report suspicions of child abuse and neglect. However, the following professionals are **required** to report:
   "Any attorney, physician, . . . dentist, podiatrist, registered or licensed practical nurse, or other health care professional, licensed psychologist, speech pathologist . . . administrator or employee of a child day-care center . . . or a certified child care agency or other public or private children services agency, school teacher or school authority, . . . **or person rendering spiritual treatment through prayer in accordance with the tenets of a well recognized religion [clergy],** acting in his official or professional capacity having reason to believe that a child less than eighteen years of age or any crippled or otherwise physically or mentally handicapped child under twenty-one years of age has suffered any wound, injury, disability, or condition of such a nature as to reasonably indicate abuse or neglect of the child shall immediately report or

cause reports to be made of such information."[2]

Ohio law further states: "Any person who is required to report cases of child abuse or neglect may take or cause to be taken color photographs of areas of trauma visible on a child, and if medically indicated, cause to be performed radiological examinations of the child."[3]

"Anyone or any . . . institution . . . or agency participating in the making of the reports, or anyone participating in a judicial proceeding resulting from the reports, shall be immune from any civil or criminal liability that might otherwise be incurred or imposed as a result of such action."[4]

Failure to make a report of suspected child abuse can result in a fine and/or sentence for professionals who are specifically required to make reports.

"In accordance with Section 2151.99 of the Revised Code, when any person acting in his official or professional capacity . . . is mandated to immediately report alleged child abuse and neglect and 'recklessly' fails to do so, the PCSA shall give written notification of such failure to the county prosecutor or city director of law. A copy of the written notification shall be retained in the case record."

"Recklessly failing to report child abuse and neglect, when required to do so in Section 2151.421 . . . is a misdemeanor of the fourth degree."[5]

III. Child Abuse Consultation Team

Few cases of child abuse are black and white. Allegations are usually based on suspicion, and abusers often deny any wrongdoing. It is often unclear whether or not a situation should be reported. Thus it is important that a well-trained multi-disciplinary team confer together about suspected cases and make a joint decision as to the best course of action.

A report of suspected child abuse should be directed to _____ , who will then call an emergency meeting of the consultation team. The team will consist of:

_____ , Minister

_____ , Chairman of the Board

_____ , Psychologist

_____ , Nurse

_____ , Child Abuse Consultant

_____ , Addictions Counselor

Attorney _____ will not be a member of the team, but will serve as legal counsel.

The reporter will present the case to the team, who will ask questions and gather more information if necessary. The team will make a timely decision as to whether or not to make an official report, and how best to help the victim, family, members, and abuser.

Confidentiality will be strictly maintained by all members.

IV. Reporting Procedure

_____ will telephone the Child Protective Services Department of Warren County, 933–1500. The authorities will assume responsibility for investigating the case. The team will cooperate with the investigation however possible. No contact will be made with the alleged abuser until the alleged victim's safety is assured.

_____ will file a written report to CPS

within 24 hours, including A) names and addresses of the child and his parents or custodian if known, B) the child's age and nature and extent of injuries, abuse, or neglect, including any evidence, and C) any other information which might be helpful in establishing the cause of the abuse or neglect.

_____ will follow up with CPS to keep apprised of the status of the investigation and proceedings.

Note:

Warren County CPS employs a deputy who is specially trained to conduct joint investigations in sexual abuse cases or other cases which might involve criminal pro-ceedings. _____ , the CPS Supervisor for Warren Co., will be consulted if there is a question as to whether or not a case should be reported.

V. Follow Up

The consultation team will see that counseling or other necessary services are provided for the victim and his/her family. In most cases, the authorities will take care of this, but the team will "watch dog" to be sure that the victim and family have as much help as they need.

Every effort will be made to help the victim, family, and if applicable, the abuser, to be healed and restored emotionally and spiritually.

VI. Staff Screening

Informal, discreet attention will be given during inter-views to try to assess if a potential employee appears to be at risk of abuse.

All staff members will be asked to read this policy.

VII. Teacher and Youth Worker Education

All teachers and other volunteers who work with children and youth will be asked to read this policy. A copy of abuse indicators and guidelines for proper response to a disclosure of abuse will be given to volunteers.

Periodic training will be provided on the topic of child abuse.

Volunteers should never use any form of physical discipline with children and youth who are not their own children. Proper disciplinary measures should be discussed with department supervisors. Touching children in warm, appropriate ways is strongly encouraged (pats on the back, hugs, etc.). However, volunteers should take care to never touch children and youth inappropriately or sexually (kissing on the mouth, touching any private part, close, full body embraces, "slaps on the bottom," etc.) Such inappropriate touching might be interpreted as abuse by a witness, even if no abuse was intended.

1. "Child Abuse and Neglect," Ohio Dept. of Human Services, Office of Compliance and Review, 1988, p. 11, 12.

2. "State of Ohio: The Abused and Neglected Child Reporting Law," Ohio Public Dept. of Public Welfare, 1979.

3. State of Ohio, *ibid.*

4. State of Ohio, *ibid.*

5. Ohio Revised Code, Children's Protective Services, Chapter 3000, 3103, OAC Cite: 5101:2–34–04.

A well-developed plan for addressing child abuse will probably be well received by church members as long as church leaders take care not to make it a central focus that might seem threatening or cause paranoia in the congregation. *The goal is to prevent child abuse, not to launch a "witch hunt" for all those who have ever raised their voices at a child.* Neither should there be any suggestion that parents do not have the right to spank their own children as a disciplinary measure. Abuse prevention strategies should be slowly and methodically incorporated in the total church education and family support programs.

If your consultation team determines that a suspected case of abuse should be reported to the authorities, they should follow the procedure outlined in the model policy. Leave the questioning to trained authorities. Too much interrogation by untrained adults can be more detrimental than helpful. It is crucial that the child not be "led" to make particular statements.

In most cases, it is difficult to determine whether or not the allegations are true. Do not confront the accused with knowledge about abuse until the child's safety has been insured. Denial is the usual response, and it may take a skilled investigator to learn the truth.

As a safeguard for everyone concerned, the accused individual should be isolated from other children until the investigation has been completed.

The person who reports the abuse will probably not be called upon to testify in court unless he or she actually witnessed the abuse.

Face the Challenge

Christians must face child abuse as a harsh reality. However, it is not a hopeless problem! The abuse prevention strategies discussed have been proven to work. The challenge for Christians is to go beyond trying to prevent bad things from happening to some children. We must work to make good things happen for all children.

First, examine attitudes toward children in your church. Are children respected and treated with sensitivity? Are their needs provided for? Is the nursery adequate? What importance is placed on the children's education programs? Are your teens valued? Are they nurtured and given opportunities for growth?

Then encourage a greater awareness of child abuse. Approach the church board, the staff, and the entire congregation to offer ideas about what can be done. Of course your church will not do all these things by next week or even by next year, but you can start some abuse prevention measures right away. Set up an advisory board to decide what the church can do.

God will bless your efforts. All your work to protect His little ones and strengthen family relationships in your congregation and community will bring great reward — for the children, for the families, for the church, and for the kingdom.

How does the problem of child abuse and neglect gain the attention of church leaders and members? Unfortunately, it often takes a devastating case of abuse to motivate a congregation to action. However, the catalyst can be one individual member who bears a burden for troubled children and their families. Free or inexpensive training is available in most communities. Many doctors, nurses, social workers, teachers, counselors, and law enforcement personnel have been specially trained about child abuse and can serve as professional consultants or educators. Community organizations such as the Mental Health Association, government agencies such as the Children's Protective Services Department, or the local children's hospital might provide training on child abuse.

Consider developing a policy and programming to educate your staff, workers, parents and children. It's a matter of moral and legal responsibility!

CHAPTER TEN

How Can Parents Reduce the Risk of Sexual Victimization for their Children?

Teaching children personal body safety is probably the best defense parents can give them against sexual abuse. However, parents and caretakers can take precautions to provide increased protection for their children. Although not an inexhaustible list of dos and don'ts, the following suggestions will reduce the risk of sexual molestation by someone outside a child's own family.

(1) *Never leave a child alone in one part of a store while you shop in another.* More than one child has been abducted from a toy department where parents had left him for only a few minutes.

(2) *Do not allow your child to go into a public restroom alone.* If your child is the opposite sex, and too old to go in the restroom with you, stand just outside the door. Tell your

child to yell if she/he encounters a problem. Don't hesitate to go in if your child yells or if she/he is in there too long. Your child's safety is more important than propriety!

(3) *Similarly never leave children alone in a car while you run into a store, no matter how convenient it may seem.* The convenience just isn't worth the risk.

(4) *Do not let very young children play alone, even in your own yard unless it is securely enclosed and protected.* Children under five do not stop to think about rules when they are attracted by activities outside their defined boundaries, and they will often wander off.

If you have a dog, use that trusted friend to help protect your children while they are in the yard. When children are not supervised, ask them to report in regularly. Check on them yourself frequently. Older children can be given responsibility to see that younger ones do not stray, and to report anything out of the ordinary they see in the neighborhood. They should be taught to come tell you if someone they do not know asks for help or tries to strike up a conversation. They need not be rude, but they can simply say, "Just a minute, please, I'll go get my mother/father. She/he can help you better than I can."

It is not a good policy to allow children to wander freely back and forth between houses. Parents should know exactly where their children are.

(5) *Older children may be permitted more freedom, but always exercise caution in allowing them to walk somewhere alone. If at all possible, children should be accompanied by an adult or another child.* They should call home when they have arrived at their destination. Don't allow much time to elapse before you start checking on your child's whereabouts if the call isn't received when it should be. Your child will

soon learn that he had better not dawdle between points!

Also, if your child will play or spend the night at a friend's house, find out what you can about the family without becoming a "busybody." Take your child to the home or pick him up several times to learn how the parents treat their own children. Are they concerned about where their children are? Be genuinely friendly, and take care not to appear suspicious.

(6) *Stay with young children during doctor visits unless there is a very good reason for not doing so.* If asked to leave, be alert to the child's behavior afterward. Ask them to tell you exactly what the doctor did. *(As with all such questioning, ask in an interested rather than suspicious way so that your child does not become alarmed or fearful of the individual. For example, don't say "Did that doctor try anything with you?" Instead, ask a series of questions to find out how the doctor conducted the examination: "What did he do first?" "How did he listen to your heart?" "What did he do after that?" and so on. It is rare for a doctor or other health care professional to molest children, but it does happen occasionally.)*

(7) *It is truly worth the effort to locate responsible, trustworthy babysitters.* Try to learn all you can about anyone with whom you leave your children! Before the sitter comes, give children permission to call a neighbor if the babysitter asks them to do something they know they should not do. Never tell them to do "whatever the sitter says." When possible, see that the children are already bathed and ready for bed. Repeat the house rules to the babysitter in front of your children. This reduces the risk of manipulation. Explain that young children are ready for bed, that older children are capable of getting ready for bed alone, that baths are not necessary, and so on. Specify which, if any, television shows may be watched, as well as which ones are prohibited. Stress that children are not

to stay up later than the specified bedtime, and that no one else is to be allowed to come in the house. Leave telephone numbers and instructions for emergencies. Responsible babysitters will understand your concerns and should not be offended by your precautious attitude. If you child is overly uneasy about staying with a particular sitter try to find out why.

Establish a code word with your child that can be used to indicate something is wrong without raising suspicion on the part of the sitter. For example, you might use a pet's name or a favorite doll's name as a code. Call home when your child is with a sitter and ask to speak with your child to make certain everything is OK. If the child is experiencing trouble, he can say "I don't think Rover is very happy." Then you can either ask questions, have your child call a neighbor or come home immediately, depending on the circumstances. Naturally you will have to teach your child how to use the code, along with when it is appropriate to use it.

(8) *Teach your child how to handle telephone calls if she is left alone at home.* She should never reveal she is home alone. She can say, "My parents can't come to the phone right now, but they'll call you back. May I have your name and phone number please?" You might even type this message on a card and tape it near your phone. Instruct your child to hang up if the caller pushes for more information, then to call a neighbor or someone else for help. Likewise, train your child not to answer the door when you aren't home, and to call for help if the individual doesn't go away. If at all possible, do not leave your child home alone!

(9) *Become involved in organizations and programs your children participate in.* This checklist for preschool and day-care center evaluation could be used for other child organizations as well:

- Does the preschool have a good reputation? Is it licensed by the state or locally? Is it recommended by a referral service or other community agencies? What do other parents think of the program?
- How are employees hired? Are backgrounds thoroughly checked? *(Some states permit employers to check the State's Central Registry to see if child-care workers have ever been reported for child abuse.)*
- How open are the teachers or staff to parent participation? What is the attitude and degree of openness? Do they encourage communication? Would they welcome an unscheduled visit?
- How carefully are the children supervised? What are the requirements for permitting a child to leave with someone besides the usual caretaker? *(Children should never be released to anyone without written authorization other than the parent or caretaker.)*

(10) *Many schools have a policy of calling the home of a child who is absent.* This safety check is especially important for children who must wait for a bus or walk to school. Parents can organize a volunteer calling system if schools cannot provide this service.

(11) *Photograph your child annually. Police agencies usually provide free fingerprinting of children.* Keep the photo and prints in a safe place for quick access in case your child disappears.

Although personalized T-shirts and sweaters are fun to wear, experts caution that they permit abductors to easily gain access to a young child. If your child wishes to wear personalized clothing, make certain he wears it on days that you will be with him. Older children who understand that they should be wary of strangers who call them by name may be permitted to wear personalized sport shirts and jackets.

Law enforcement agencies recommend that children carry a concealed ID card with emergency phone money taped to the back. Or they can wear a dog tag under their clothing. It is also a good idea to mark the child's name on the inside of sweaters and other wearing apparel.

(12) *Pay careful attention if your child doesn't want to be with a particular person.* Encourage him to express his reasons and feelings. Even when the cause for anxiety is not sexual abuse, the child will be validated by your respect and recognition of his rights.

(13) *Make it clear to your children that you want to help them whenever they are hurt, in trouble, or upset, even if their problem happened as a result of their breaking a rule.* Adolescents often find themselves in potentially dangerous situations, but they may fear chastisement from home so much that they are afraid to call. Children should never fear punishment so much that they will not ask for help with their problems.

Encourage your child to call home anytime he feels afraid or uncomfortable. Assure him that you will come to his rescue immediately, no matter where he is. Young children should be taught how to use all kinds of phones and be given emergency phone money.

Prepare Yourself for Teaching Personal Body Safety Skills!

"Askable" parents who are readily available enjoy the best relationships with their children. A child whose mother and father are open to any discussion, and who are genuinely interested in his activities and friends, is indeed a fortunate child. Think for a moment about the amount of "quality time" you spend with each of your children per day. Time spent watching television, "wolfing down" family meals, barking commands, working independently, or even sitting together in the same room does not count! "Quality time" refers to time devoted specifically and wholly to a two-way communication between you and your child.

Dr. Sidney Lecher, child psychiatrist, maintains that parents can achieve a healthy, supportive relationship with their children when they spend as little as twenty minutes per day with them, as long as that time is "quality time." The "school of hard knocks" that so many children grow up in leaves a lot to be desired in the development of a mature, well-rounded adult. Each day try to teach your child one little trick of adulthood that he will probably not learn on his own or at school. Praise his achievements, help him learn from his failures, and respect his opinions and worries. If children feel they can talk to you about minor problems, they will be more likely to tell you about the major ones.

Before you begin teaching your child about personal body safety, invest some time in self-examination. Pray, meditate, and read what the Bible says about sexuality. Make an honest assessment of your own attitudes about sex. Many Christian authors have written books on the subject that might help if your feelings are unclear. If you have committed an act of sexual immortality as an adult, come clean before the Lord, repent, and ask for forgiveness before beginning to teach your child about sexuality. If you were sexually abused as a child, or if some experience has left you extremely uncomfortable, try to confront any unresolved feelings. A number of middle-aged adults have been freed of depression, fear and guilt when they finally talked about their sexual victimization as children. Don't be ashamed or embarrassed to seek counseling or therapy if you are harboring depressing memories.

Asking for help is a sign of courage, not weakness.

Educate yourself about the problem of child sexual abuse by reading articles and books available on the subject. This book provides enough basic information about sexual abuse to enable you to train your child adequately.

Do Yourself and Your Child a Favor by Teaching Her About Sexuality Before She Learns It on Her Own!

Children of all ages need knowledge about sexuality. Even toddlers with limited vocabularies should be taught the names of the parts of their bodies. It is inconsistent to teach a child that she has ears and toes and leave out the parts in between. The child's activity book refers to a child's breast and genitalia as "private parts," and explains that "private parts" are those body parts that are covered when a child wears a swimsuit.

The age at which you begin teaching your child about sexuality is of course your own choice. Some parents begin very early, reasoning that the more a child knows about sex, the less she will be enticed by her curiosity about the "secret subject." Many parents feel that it is sufficient to teach three-four- and five-year-aids concepts about "good, bad, and sexual touches." They stress that no one has a right to touch or look at their private parts. It is very important that all young children know at least this much. When taught within the context of other safety skills in a nonfrightening way, most preschoolers understand this very well.

Although most of today's parents realize that sex education is important, many feel uneasy about initiating the topic. They often wait for questions from their children before discussing it. Children who are accustomed to communicating with their parents may well ask about sex, but many children will never bring up the subject.

It is vitally important that children learn that God's plan for sexuality includes far more than physical sensations and reproduction facts. The lessons we so want our children to learn about sexuality — love, affection, fidelity, and responsibility to one's partner in marriage — are best communicated by the living example of Christian parents that a child sees within his own home. If you are a single parent, you will need to sensitively explain why your spouse is not in your house. Ask your minister or a Christian friend to assist you if you don't know what to say to your child.

Consider teaching your child about sexuality while she is young enough not to have been exposed to too much talk about it among her friends. If you begin early enough, you will have the advantage of setting your own timing and environment for this very important instruction. The "best" age for this instruction varies with different families and children. Be aware that most children will be exposed to discussions about sex before age nine — many much earlier. Keep in mind, too, that child molesters seek children who are ignorant about sexuality.

Refrain from reacting with shock and disgust the first time your child repeats an obscene sexual word he has heard at school or in the neighborhood. Rather, seize the teachable moment! Define the word in a way that the child can understand. Teach the appropriate word, along with instructions about when she may or may not use it.

An illustration of how "askable" parents seized the teachable moment follows:

"We were surprised when our seven-year-old daughter asked at dinner one night about the meaning of what she referred to as the 'f-word.' She had heard the word used by children on the school bus, and she already knew without our

telling her that it was not a word to be verbalized! We looked at one another, neither of us really wanting to explain the whole subject at that moment in front of our three-year-old. But we knew that a dismissal of the question would be the wrong response.

"Mother was the first to speak. 'Although the f-word is not a nice word to use, it means something very special that Daddy and I want to tell you about. Can you wait until tomorrow night? You, Daddy and I will have a conversation about the f-word after your sister has gone to bed.'

"We felt bad about putting her off but we wanted a chance to plan our approach. We had been caught off guard and felt unprepared. Happily she accepted our procrastination, and eagerly awaited the next evening's conversation.

"After praying together for the Lord's guidance, we decided not only to answer our child's specific question, but to outline the entire concept of sexuality as planned by God: how a man and woman fall in love and marry, how they express their love emotionally and physically, and how babies are conceived and born. After that we would educate her about the sinful distortion of God's plan by many in the world explaining that sometimes people engage in sexual intercourse when they are not married. We had discussed personal body safety with her when she was younger, and we had taught her to say no if anyone tried to touch her private parts. Now we would define the dangers more specifically. We didn't consider that all that information might be too much for one sitting!

"We borrowed a book from the library to help with our lesson. Since it had not been written with a Christian's perspective, we added the explanation about God's plan.

"We began by asking questions to find out how much our

child already knew. When asked the meaning of 'sex,' she replied 'it's when you kiss someone and act like a hotshot.' Upon further questioning, we discovered that her knowledge did not go beyond the vague notions she had expressed. We felt fortunate to have the opportunity to teach her together about love in the context of God's plan. We were glad that the information she would have about sexuality would be accurate and would come from parents who love her.

"We encouraged her to ask questions as we went along. Although we tried to present the information logically and completely, it was necessary to backtrack, reexplain, and clarify points. It was a great deal for her to absorb! She found it hard to understand why anyone could ever want to engage in sexual intercourse. Although we assured her that someday she would understand that feeling better, we were pleased that she wanted no part of it for the present!

"We reinforced and expanded this instruction in the weeks and months that followed."

The best way to insure that you will have a similar opportunity to teach your child about sexuality is to plan ahead. If possible, obtain one of the many books available for Christian parents and children on sex education. Choose a convenient, appropriate time and initiate the topic yourself. No doubt it will be one of the lasting memories in your child's life.

Now You're Ready to Teach Personal Body Safety to the Children You Care About!

Include personal body safety instruction with other personal safety issues. Topics of fire and poison safety, street rules, sharp and hot objects, and so on should be linked with the concept of self-protection skills. Knowledge about emergency phone skills, and how to seek help from police officers, teachers, neighbors, church members, and family members also apply to the topic of personal body safety. By including protection from sexual abuse with the broad concept of safety, children will be less apt to become paranoid about every unknown person they encounter. Enlightened children will be better able to recognize danger and avoid violence and abuse.

Just as other safety instructions change as your child grows older, the specifics you teach your child about personal body safety will change. *(For example: A toddler is told "Don't go near the street"; a first grader, "Look both ways before crossing"; an eight-year-old, "When walking on a road, face oncoming traffic.")* He may begin with an awareness that it is wrong for anyone to touch his private parts, and that he should tell if they do. As he grows older the type of touching will need further explanation. Before adolescence, children should fully understand the danger of sexual abuse, so they can resist the lures of prostitution and pornography frequently directed at their natural rebelliousness and yearning for independence. Be sure to include discussions about AIDS and abortion, emphasizing Christian values.

Tell your child that together you are going to study some very important ideas. Choose a place and time that will provide the opportunity for as much concentration as possible, and BEGIN! *(These lessons are also suitable for small group instruction.)*

PARENTS/TEACHERS GUIDE

This teaching guide is intended for use with the pupil activity book, *Good Hugs and Bad Hugs.*

Page 3
Objective: To install a confidence in your child that God loves him just the way he is.
Children need to be reminded again and again that God loves them for themselves. Assure your child that you, too, love him just the way he is. If he is sure of God's love and your love, he can become more sure of his own capabilities and develop a high self-esteem.

I AM SPECIAL TO GOD!

Jesus called the _____ *to him and said, "Let the little come to me, and do not hinder them, for the* _____ *of* _____ *belongs to such as these."* —Luke 18:16

God loves _____ .
(your name)

He gave me a MIND and a BODY that is not like anyone else's. He wants me to use my MIND and my BODY to honor Him.

I praise you because I am fearfully and _____ *made; your* _____ *are wonderful. I know that full well.* —Psalm 139:14

I am custom-made by God.

PRESENTING . . .   (NAME)

Draw a picture that shows what you look like.

3

139

Locate the Bible verses together. Ask your child to read the verses and fill in the blanks. *(Answers: children, children, kingdom, God; wonderfully, works.)* Younger children should be able to understand the meanings of the verses when explained.

As your child draws a picture of himself, help him to focus on his positive characteristics. Minimize any physical or developmental shortcomings. Praise his work!

Extra Activity: Review picture albums together that trace your child's growth. Help him to feel good about his physical development. Spend lots of time sharing memories together.

Page 4

Objective: To help build your child's self-esteem and a sense of pride for her accomplishments.

Children with low self-esteem are more vulnerable to child sexual molestation, as well as other social dangers such as alcohol or drug abuse, than

I CAN DO MANY THINGS

Make a list or draw pictures of the things you are good at or just like to do.

4

children who are confident enough to stand up for themselves.

Before beginning this lesson, ask your family *(or class)* to take turns saying one kind thing about each person in the group. "I like *(name)* because . . ." Then talk about how nice it feels to receive a compliment. Next, ask each person to complete the sentence, "I like myself because . . ."

You may need to help your child begin thinking about things she does well. Encourage her to talk about specific experiences as she completes the activity page. With encouragement, she will probably soon have plenty to say! Be generous with sincere praise!

Extra Activities: Help your child decorate a pocket mirror or hand mirror that she may keep in her own room. Use decals or paint to make a design on one side — such as a rainbow and heart. Put narrow strips of adhesive tape on the mirror's top and bottom. Print, "I am special to God."

Make an "All About *(Name)*" booklet or collage. Your child can draw pictures, use photos, or cut out magazine pictures to represent her positive characteristics.

GOD WANTS ME TO BE SAFE

I need to use my MIND to keep my BODY safe from harm.

What could your MIND tell you to do to help keep your BODY safe in each picture below?

5

141

Help your child write a letter to a relative or friend in another town, telling all about a recent accomplishment.

Page 5
Objective: To illustrate how your child can use his mind to help him avoid danger.

It is important not to frighten children while teaching personal body safety. The instruction flows more naturally when approached as a continuation of several safety topics.

Discuss the examples of safety precautions shown on the page with your child. Give him an opportunity to express his thoughts about what to do in each situation. You may want to relate some personal experience you have had in which you avoided danger by using your head.

Ask your child to think of other instances in which he can use his mind to avoid danger. *(Do not yet discuss "stranger danger" or sexual abuse at great length.)*

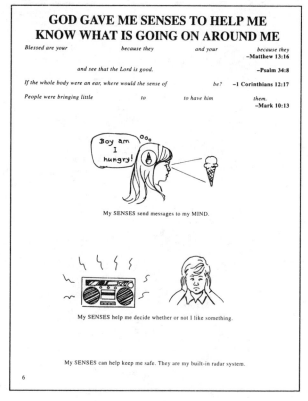

Pages 6 and 7
Objective: To help your child become familiar with or review the five senses, and how they help us to recognize danger.
Children need to realize that their senses often warn them of danger. They should be encouraged to trust their instincts when something seems to be wrong, even when they don't know exactly what the problem is.

As your child searches to find the Scripture verses, point out the sounds, sights, and smells you notice at that very moment. *(Answers: eyes, see, ears, hear; taste; smell; children, Jesus, touch.)*

Older children may be interested in studying a drawing of the human brain, with a scientific explanation of how sensory messages are sent through the nervous system. Check your local library for an appropriate book about the human body.

Younger children will better understand what their senses are by actually using each sense in a fun way. Make a guessing game of tasting, hearing, smelling, seeing, and touching unusual or favorite things.

1. Draw a line and match each SENSE with the correct body part.
2. Draw a line and match each SENSE with the picture that shows how it can help keep you safe.
3. Circle the one SENSE that uses your whole body.

TOUCHING

SMELLING

TASTING

HEARING

SEEING

143

Discuss examples of things children like and dislike based on the message received by a sense *(a skunk's odor, soothing music, etc.)*.

Discuss the examples shown in the pictures with your child while he completes the matching activity. Discuss other examples that demonstrate a sense of danger.

Extra Activity: Make a poster or table display that depicts the five senses in a way chosen by your child. *(It could be a scientific illustration of how senses work, a collage of likes and dislikes based on sensory information, a chart listing examples of each kind of sense, a drawing of your child that shows him using his senses in some way, or anything else your child desires.)*

Continue to reinforce your child's use of his senses at every opportunity during the next few days.

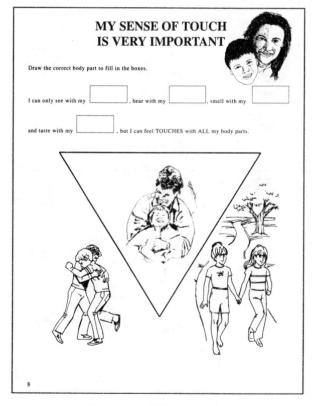

Pages 8 and 9
Objective: To focus on the sense of touch, and to introduce the idea that there are many kinds of touches.
Children need to understand what kinds of touches are good and what kinds are bad, so they will be better able to distinguish sexual exploitation from healthy affection.

Discuss the examples of touch shown as your child completes the activity. Draw upon your child's personal experiences whenever possible.

Page 10
Objective: To assure your child that God wants people to touch others in ways that make them feel happy and good.
It is vitally important that people do not stop expressing affection for children as a reaction to a fear of being accused of sexual molestation. It is equally important that children do not stop accepting and giving affection. Both children and adults need lots of love, expressed through warm hugs,

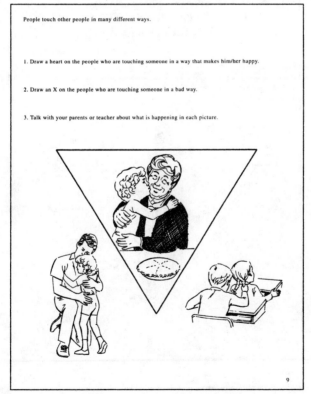

People touch other people in many different ways.

1. Draw a heart on the people who are touching someone in a way that makes him/her happy.

2. Draw an X on the people who are touching someone in a bad way.

3. Talk with your parents or teacher about what is happening in each picture.

9

kisses, pats, snuggles, and other good touches!

As your child colors the picture, talk about good touches. Begin by reading and discussing Mark 10:13-16. *(Answers: arms, hands.)* Ask your child to name the kinds of touches that make him feel good. Discuss specific examples, and add your own experiences with good touches *(kisses, hugs, snuggles, cuddles, handshakes, holding hands, back rubs, pats on the back, love pats, pats of comfort, and fun tickles).*

Extra Activities: Role play good touches with children in one of the following ways:

Younger children will especially enjoy doll or puppet role plays of good touches. Older children can perform a role play themselves. In classroom settings, some children may feel embarrassed at demonstrating good touches on one another. If so, have children demonstrate good touches on a stuffed animal or doll, or other well-liked inanimate object. Fourth to sixth graders may think it more fun to hug out of the ordinary objects such as a chair or broom. If these methods are used, stress that you are talking about

GOD WANTS PEOPLE TO TOUCH EACH OTHER IN GOOD WAYS

He (Jesus) took the children in his   *put his*   *on them and blessed them.*
                                                      –Mark 10:16

Snuggles, hugs, and kisses from those we love make us happy.

While you color this picture, name all the good touches you can think of.

BIBLE STORIES

10

146

touching between people.

First pretend you are a grandparent *(or other adult relative outside the immediate family)*. Ask your child to show how he could touch the grand-parent in a good way. Show a response to touches to indicate happiness. Then pretend you are the child, and he is the relative. Have him show ways that he would like to be touched by the relative. Act out other situations involving individuals within the immediate family — a friend, a well-liked teacher, and so on. Include other adults who are known and liked, but not known very well.

Page 11
Objective: To help your child identify how she felt when she was touched in a good way, and to want to touch others in good ways.

Ask your child to draw a picture of someone touching her in a good way. Remind her to draw facial expressions that show how good she felt. Encourage her to think of adjectives and phrases that describe her good

**GOOD TOUCHES
MAKE ME FEEL GOOD**

Draw a picture that shows when
someone touched you in a good way.

How did you feel when the person touched you this way?

11

feelings *(loved, wanted to be touched again, unafraid, happy, warm, wanted to do something nice for the person, etc.).*

Page 12
Objective: To help your child remember how he felt when someone touched him in a bad way, and to teach him it is usually wrong to touch others in these ways. *(Keep in mind that self-defense may be necessary in some instances.)*
Many children know all too well how bad it feels to be pushed, shoved, hit, bitten, kicked, slapped, or pinched, for these behaviors happen often on school playgrounds, in neighborhoods, and sometimes within families. Do not encourage role play of bad touches between people.)

Read the Bible verses together. Then talk about the meaning of the "Golden Rule." (Answer: *others, you.*)

Discuss examples of bad touches, including the ones mentioned above. Unless your child initiates the discussion, postpone the topic of sexual

---

SOME TOUCHES DO NOT FEEL GOOD

Sometimes people do not touch others in the ways that God wants them to. They do not follow the Golden Rule:
"In everything, do to   *what you would have them do to*   *."*–**Matthew 7:12**

Draw a picture that shows when someone touched you in a way that you did not like.

Describe how you felt when the person touched you this way.

_____

_____

_____

12

---

touching. Discuss his sad feelings as he draws a picture of when he was touched in a bad way. Talk also about how others may have felt when your child touched them in a bad way.

Page 13
Objective: To help your child understand why she sometimes feels uncomfortable when someone touches her in what may be considered a good touch or at least not a "bad touch."

An appropriate touch from a family member may be inappropriate by someone outside the family. Too often children are subjected to cuddles and kisses by well-meaning adults they do not know well. Many parents not only condone it, but encourage their children to accept such affection. ("Uncle Charlie may remember you in his will!") Try to imagine how YOU would feel if a casual business acquaintance or even a neighbor came up and pinched your cheek or planted a kiss on YOUR lips! Children need to be granted the right to graciously refuse unwelcome affection and be taught

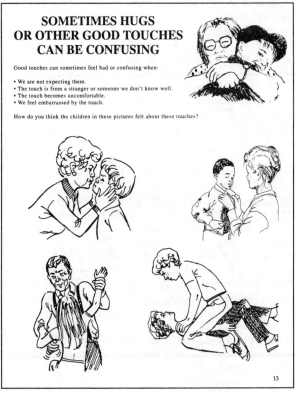

149

how to do so nonoffensively.

Read the description for each picture. Then ask your child how she thinks each child felt, and what she would advise him/her to do.

- Mary's grandfather loved to tease her, and sometimes Mary enjoyed his teasing. He especially like to tickle her. Mary thought a little tickling was fun, and she would usually giggle for a minute or two. Sometimes, though, her grandfather didn't know when to stop. Mary didn't like it when her grandfather tickled her for a long time. Mary stopped laughing and tried to squirm away, but her grandfather held her tight and kept right on tickling. She was afraid to ask him to stop.

- Jerry loved to wrestle with his cousin Bob. Jerry was pretty good, even though Bob was several years older. Once when they were wrestling, though, Bob had to try so hard to pin Jerry down that he became very rough. Jerry didn't want to admit that Bob was hurting him, so he just kept on trying to break Bob's holds. He could hardly keep from crying when Bob threw him down hard, then sat on him. "Hey, you're not going to be a crybaby, are you?" Bob laughed. "I thought you liked to wrestle with me!"

- Carl's Aunt Marie, who lived far away, decided to come to visit his family. Carl had seen her a few times, but she always sent him presents on his birthday. "Be nice to Aunt Marie," Carl's mother said. *I'll just have to grit my teeth and bear it when she arrives,* he thought to himself. Sure enough, as soon as she walked in the door, Aunt Marie put her hands on both his cheeks and gave him a wet kiss right on the lips.

- Lucy and her mother were shopping in a department store when her mother spotted an old friend that she had not seen for a long time. Lucy had never met her, but her mother's friend looked very nice. "Marty, I'd like you to meet my daughter Lucy," said her mother. Suddenly Marty picked Lucy up and hugged her tightly. "What a big girl!" she exclaimed.

Share with your child an example of a time when you were uncomfortable by a touch from someone. Encourage her to talk about a time when she felt uncomfortable. If your child expresses discomfort at being expected to hug a relative or other person close to your family, discuss her feelings. Perhaps you can help her understand that hugging the person makes him/her very happy, and help her to feel more comfortable. On the other hand, if she is very uncomfortable, give some suggestions as to how she can graciously refuse the affection. *(See discussion for page 14.)*

Page 14
Objectives: To help your child learn that her body is her own, and that she has the right to speak up if someone is touching her in a way she

does not like; to provide an example of how to handle unwanted affection.

It is important to point out to children that although you want them to respect and obey their elders, you do not expect them to allow adults to touch them in ways they do not like. An especially difficult situation arises when relatives or friends who are not well-known or liked by the child want to give and receive affection. You can explain to your child how much the relative likes her, and that it would make the relative happy if she could show some affection, such as giving Uncle Frank a kiss on the cheek. However, do not force your child to put up with affection that is too much for her. Make it clear to your child that she doesn't have to do everything an adult asks.

Look together at the pictures on page 13 again. Discuss how the children receiving the touches felt. Then read the story about Sharon. Ask your child to repeat what Sharon said to Uncle Frank. Then ask her to fill in the answer to the question about what she would say.

MY BODY BELONGS TO ME

Read 1 Corinthians 6:20.
I can use my MIND to try to stop touches I do not like.

Look back at the pictures on page 13. The children in these pictures did not like the touches they were receiving.

Sharon had a problem like this, too. Every time Uncle Frank came to visit, he would pick her up and squeeze her tightly. Sometimes he kissed her on the lips and asked her to give him a kiss. Sharon liked Uncle Frank, but she hated the way he hugged and kissed her. She wished he would stop. Sharon knew that God wanted her to feel happy when someone touched her. But Uncle Frank's hugs and kisses made her feel bad.

One day she decided to do something about it. As soon as he picked her up, she said, "Uncle Frank, I'm happy to see you, but would you please put me down? I do not like to be squeezed so hard." It was a difficult thing to say, but Sharon was glad she had said it.

Uncle Frank was surprised. He put her down and apologized. "Sharon, I only hugged and kissed you because I like you so much. But if you really don't want me to do that, I won't. How about if we just shake hands?"

Sharon smiled. "Thank you, Uncle Frank, for understanding how I feel."

If someone touches me in a way I don't like, I have the right to say,

_____

14

151

Pages 15 and 16
Objectives: To teach your child names for his genitalia; to initiate a discussion about sexual touches; to help him clearly understand when touching of his private parts by an adult or adolescent is acceptable and when it is not.*This topic needs to be handled very sensitively! While children must be taught that sexual touches from adults or adolescents are wrong, they should never be made to feel ashamed of their private parts, or that these parts of their body are dirty. Be careful not to create guilty feelings about their sexuality that might cause trouble for them as marriage partners. Although the topic is not covered in this book, we suggest that sexuality education be taught to children before they reach age nine, preferably earlier. Children who have been taught about God's plan for sexuality within a loving marriage will more easily understand the concept of sexual abuse. Younger children can be taught about bad touches without knowing all about sexuality.*

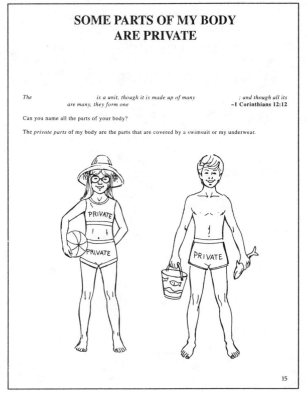

SOME PARTS OF MY BODY
ARE PRIVATE

The _____ is a unit, though it is made up of many _____; and though all its are many, they form one _____ –1 Corinthians 12:12

Can you name all the parts of your body?

The *private parts* of my body are the parts that are covered by a swimsuit or my underwear.

15

Locate the Bible verse and help your child fill in the missing words. *(Answers: body, parts, parts, body.)* Ask your child to name the body parts on the drawings as you point to them *(arm, nose, etc.).* As you discuss "private parts," refer to them by the accepted terms in your family. *(If "baby-ish" words have been used before now, consider teaching your child different terms.)* The correct terms are breast, vagina, and penis. Some parents prefer that young children simply use the term "private parts." Ask your child about terms he has heard others use. Take the opportunity to help him understand why he should not use vulgar or inappropriate terms.

Talk about times when it's OK for an adult to touch a child's private parts *(changing diapers, medicating for rashes, sores or redness, bathing young children, physician's checkup).* Help your child list some examples on the blank lines.

Discuss the fact that sometimes adults do things that are wrong. Mention burglaries and other examples of sinful behavior your child can understand. Go on to explain that sometimes "nice" people, even people your child may

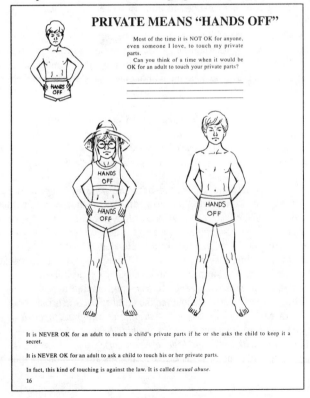

PRIVATE MEANS "HANDS OFF"

Most of the time it is NOT OK for anyone, even someone I love, to touch my private parts.

Can you think of a time when it would be OK for an adult to touch your private parts?

_____

_____

_____

HANDS OFF

HANDS OFF

HANDS OFF

HANDS OFF

It is NEVER OK for an adult to touch a child's private parts if he or she asks the child to keep it a secret.

It is NEVER OK for an adult to ask a child to touch his or her private parts.

In fact, this kind of touching is against the law. It is called *sexual abuse.*

16

know, might do something bad to him. Inform your child that some adults like to touch children's private parts or ask children to touch their private parts. Tell him that sexual touching between an adult and a child is always wrong, even if the adult is very nice and pretends that it's a game.

Use the term *sexual abuse* to mean the improper touching of private parts. Explain to your child that sexual abuse is when an adult touches or looks at his private parts, or asks him to touch or look at a private part of the adult's body. This explanation should be sufficient for youngsters who have not been taught about sex. Older children who have an understanding of sexuality may be told about rape or other forms of abuse. However, DO NOT FRIGHTEN your child by telling him gruesome details of the most severe forms of abuse. Tell only enough for him to realize the danger without becoming terrorized! Be certain that your child understands that it is wrong for any adult, including teachers, relatives, and friends, to touch him sexually.

Emphasize that this kind of problem does not happen to everyone, and that you hope it doesn't happen to him. However, tell him that if it ever does happen, you want him to know what to do.

The danger of sexual abuse will need to be reinforced in different ways at different times, for your child may become anxious at first. If you calmly reassure him and answer all his questions in a nonthreatening manner, he should be able to grasp the message without becoming frightened.

Page 17
Objective: To help your child learn how to say "no" assertively.
Sexual offenders look for cooperative victims. In most cases they will not continue sexual advances when a child resists with a firm "no." Thus, a confident refusal at the first sexual overture is a child's greatest protection against abuse!

Discuss together the difference between *passive, aggressive,* and *assertive* ways of saying "no." *Passive* refusals are not very convincing, *aggressive (mean)* refusals can lead to hostility, anger, and possible danger, while *assertive* answers express the intent to stand up for one's rights without seeking to "put down" or provoke the offender.

Role play saying "no" in the three different ways for each situation listed at the bottom of the page. Think of other examples that your child may encounter in which he needs to say "no," including situations that could lead to sexual abuse. Encourage the child to use the proper body language with each "no," *(passive — shoulders slumped, head lowered; aggressive — chin out, arms folded, provoking hostility; assertive — confident, body erect with head held high, eye contact).*

Concentrate on reinforcing assertive responses after the other types have been role played. Provide lots of practice for this very important skill!

Ways to say "no" could include "I'm not allowed to do that" if the child is in a situation that requires use of an authority figure.

Extra Activity: Bolster your child's confidence by having him practice assertive "nos" in front of a mirror.

Caution: Encourage righteous indignation, but make it clear that assertive "nos" are to be used for justifiable reasons and not childish whims! Ask your child to think of times when it is not OK to say "no."

Page 18
Objective: To teach your child to try to "get away" if someone attempts to abuse her or if she even senses danger.

Getting away from the danger of sexual abuse can be difficult for anyone, especially a small child. Spend time developing different options to use in different situations. Encourage your child to do something about it when her senses warn her about danger.

SOMETIMES I NEED TO SAY "NO!"

Saying "No!" to someone older than you are can be very hard, especially if the person is someone you like.

Pretend someone said to you, "Take off your clothes so I can teach you about the differences between boys and girls."
Of course you should say "No!" But how do you say it?
Place a check mark above the best way to say "No!" pictured below.

"No. I do not allow anyone to see or touch my private parts."

"Uh, I'd rather not do that. Uh, if you don't mind."

"You idiot! I'll punch you in the mouth if you even come near me!"

Practice saying "No!" in a confident way when your teacher or parent reads each sentence below.

● Your classmate whispers during a test, "Move your hand so I can copy your answers."
● An older and bigger student corners you in the rest room at school. "Give me your lunch money!" he (she) demands.
● While shopping with your aunt she says, "Put that cassette tape in your pocket. The salesclerk isn't watching."
● At camp while you are getting ready for bed the counselor comes and sits on your bed. He has a dirty magazine. "Look at these pictures. You'll like them," he says.

17

Review the idea that our senses often help us to know when something isn't right.

Ask your child what she thinks has happened in the picture. *(A lady the boy did not know may have asked for information, or she may have even tried to abuse him. In either case, he sensed danger, yelled "No!" and started to run away.)*

Talk about situations in which it would be possible to get away from danger. *(If a car follows her, your child can turn around and walk the other way. She can run away or tell if someone bothers her.)*

Where should your child seek help when she is in specific localities?

When should she try to fight? When shouldn't she try to fight?

Are there techniques of self-defense that your child could learn? *(This possibility depends largely on a child's size and strength. Some parents teach children to stomp on feet, bite, kick, pull hair, and punch. In some cases, such self-defense tactics will cause a molester to give up, particularly in public places. Discuss also that self-defense would probably not*

work in a confined or isolated area.)

Teach your child how to yell for help in a low, loud voice. Children's high shrieks do not attract as much attention as a clear, low, "Help, this person is not my mother (father)" or "Help, I'm being kidnapped!" Tell her to run to crowded, not isolated areas.

Finally, propose a hypothetical situation in which the molester would be someone your child knows *(Do not name an individual.)* and no one else is available to help her. In this case, she should try to get away more subtly by saying, "I want to go home now."

Page 19
Objective: To teach your child the importance of telling a trusted adult if someone exploits or tries to exploit him sexually.

Talk with your child about "good" secrets such as surprise gifts and special treats. Share some memories of past surprises for your family members. Point out that "good" secrets are usually surprises that will make someone happy, and are eventually revealed.

Then discuss together the examples mentioned on the page. While your child colors the pictures, discuss what could be happening and what the child should do about it.

Page 20
Objective: To help your child define her own support system and to encourage her to use it to help with all kinds of problems.

Before the lesson, make a list of hypothetical problems your child would need help with. Begin with examples of physical injuries. Progress to social problems with friends or siblings. Finally, role play asking for help with a problem of sexual abuse.

Begin by reading together the Bible verse and the first paragraph. *(Answers: help, trouble.)* Give an example of a time when you had a problem as a child and sought help from someone.

Then help your child develop her own support system on the umbrella. You may need to remind her of certain individuals if she doesn't think of them on her own.

Role play how she would ask for help with the problems you have listed. In at least one case, the first individual she asks should refuse to believe her or refuse to help her. This example will help her to realize that it may be necessary to ask for help more than once. Be sure to include cases in which the child is away from home and must ask help from a teacher, neighbor, clerk, or professional employee.

Extra Activities: Create your own projects to illustrate support systems. You might make collages of magazine pictures or use photos to represent certain individuals. You could draw a scene that includes a house, a school, a church building, and a few community buildings. Have your child list or draw pictures of the support people at each location.

Older children can make a problem/solution chart listing problems in one column *(hunger, a fire starts, injury, etc.)* and who to call for help in the solution column.

Page 21
Objective: To teach your child vital personal identification information.

Guide your child through each activity, helping only when needed. Sing "Jesus Loves Me" together as suggested. You may wish to make up additional verses to reinforce other information that your child should know such as business or neighbor phone numbers.

Extra Activities: Let young children help you make colorful pictures or cards that illustrate vital information. Post the cards in their room or on the

refrigerator and review them often. Reinforce vital information for older children by letting them fill out old application forms just for fun. *(Use credit applications, medical forms, and so on.)* Teach your child how to address, stamp, and mail a postcard to your home.

Page 22

Objective: To teach your child how to use various telephones and to know the person to call in case of an emergency.

Of course you don't want to teach your child to lie or be rude. However, if you leave him alone at home, he may be defenseless if he is always totally honest with callers or someone who comes to the door. Impress upon him the importance of not revealing that he is alone. Provide specific phone responses, and instructions not to open the door.

Talk about the different kinds of telephones, and provide direct experience in using each type. After completing the page together, plan a telephone field trip. You will stop at various pay phones around the community

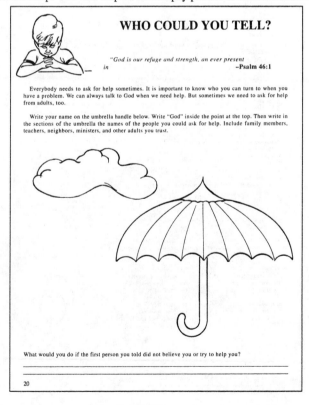

WHO COULD YOU TELL?

"God is our refuge and strength, an ever present in —**Psalm 46:1**

Everybody needs to ask for help sometimes. It is important to know who you can turn to when you have a problem. We can always talk to God when we need help. But sometimes we need to ask for help from adults, too.

Write your name on the umbrella handle below. Write "God" inside the point at the top. Then write in the sections of the umbrella the names of the people you could ask for help. Include family members, teachers, neighbors, ministers, and other adults you trust.

What would you do if the first person you told did not believe you or try to help you?

20

159

ز

and allow your child to call home. Have him practice putting in the money, dialing the operator for assistance, and dialing your own number. Additionally, teach him how to make a collect call.

"Stage" a practice call by having someone call your home and ask to speak to you. Have your child practice telling the caller, "My mother (or father) is busy and cannot come to the phone right now. Please give me your number and she'll (he'll) return your call." You might wish to tape the message above the phone so your child is not caught off guard when he receives a call while alone. If a caller continues to question him after he has given this response, tell him to hang up and call you or a neighbor immediately. While you're at it, have your child practice general telephone manners. Discuss how he should answer specific individuals or types of calls. If his experience with telephones is limited, allow many opportunities for practicing telephone use.

Let your child make a small card for emergency numbers. If he can't read, use pictures to represent numbers (*fireman's hat, policeman's hat,*

WHERE DO I BELONG?

Draw faces of yourself and the adults you live with in the circles. Can you fill in all the blanks? If not, ask your parent or teacher for help.

1. My name is _____ .
2. My father's name is _____ .
3. My mother's name is _____ .
4. If you live with someone other than your father or mother, what is his/her name? _____ .
5. Draw a picture of the house or building you live in.
6. My house or apartment number is _____ .
7. The name of the street I live on is _____ .
8. The name of the town or city I live in is _____ .
9. The name of my state is _____ .
10. My zip code is _____ .
11. My telephone number is (__ __ __) __ __ __ - __ __ __ __ .
12. My parent(s) work at _____ .
13. Emergency telephone number besides my own number (__ __ __)
    __ __ __ - __ __ __ __ .

Sing "Jesus Loves Me" with your parent or teacher. Then substitute the correct words in the song to tell important information about yourself. Follow the example below.

Jesus loves Anya Carl,
She lives at 161 Arnold Drive,
In the town of Kingston,
In the state of New York.

Jesus loves Anya Carl,
She knows how to call her home.
She dials area code 914–
339–1602.

Yes, Jesus loves her,
Yes, Jesus loves her,
Yes, Jesus loves her,
The Bible tells her so.

Yes, Jesus loves her,
Yes, Jesus loves her,
Yes, Jesus loves her,
The Bible tells her so.

21

---

ambulance, neighbor's house, your house, your place of work, and so on). Affix the card near the phone.

Page 23
Objectives: To review the important points about personal body safety that your child has studied so far; to go back over any points that she does not understand.

Help your child work the puzzle according to her reading ability. Very young children may simply tell you the answers to fill in the puzzle. Beginning readers may be able to work the puzzle with the assistance of the word list on page 31. Older children can probably work the puzzle alone.

(Answers: 1. God. 2. Mind. 3. Body. 4. Senses. 5. Feel. 6. Touch. 7. Good. 8. Bad. 9. Hugs. 10. No. 11. Private. 12. Get Away. 13. Secret. 14. Tell. 15. Telephone.)

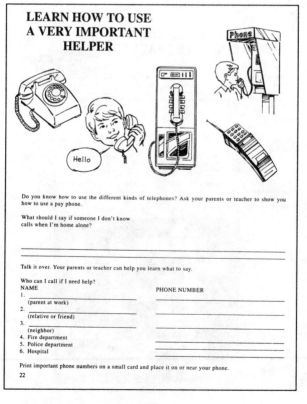

LEARN HOW TO USE A VERY IMPORTANT HELPER

Hello

Phone

Do you know how to use the different kinds of telephones? Ask your parents or teacher to show you how to use a pay phone.

What should I say if someone I don't know calls when I'm home alone?

_____

_____

Talk it over. Your parents or teacher can help you learn what to say.

Who can I call if I need help?
NAME   PHONE NUMBER
1.
 (parent at work)
2.
 (relative or friend)
3.
 (neighbor)
4. Fire department
5. Police department
6. Hospital

Print important phone numbers on a small card and place it on or near your phone.
22

Pages 24 and 25
Objectives: To present a real-life situation to your child that involves child sexual abuse; to encourage your child to use the information he has learned to help Freddy; to enlighten, not frighten!

This lesson is intended to illustrate to your child the importance of using his mind to keep his body safe. If your child has difficulty deciding what Freddy should do, very patiently review with him the primary points. Remember that your goal is to enlighten your child, not to frighten him. Emphasize that this kind of problem does not happen to everyone, and that you hope it won't ever happen to him. However, tell him that you want him to know how to handle it if it does.

Take into consideration your child's age, maturity, and level of under-standing. Use your judgment to expand upon what could happen to Freddy. If your child has been taught sexuality education, you will probably want to warn him that abuse can become more severe and frightening than gentle touching. An informed child will be less vulnerable because he will be more

DO YOU REMEMBER WHAT YOU HAVE LEARNED?

Test your memory about what you have studied so far in this book. Try to fill in the blanks of the sentences below with the correct words. Then print them in the crossword puzzle. The clues are numbered with arrows pointing down or across for the puzzle. If you have trouble, look at the word list on page 31.

1. _ _ _ _ made me, and He wants me to use my 2 _ _ _ _ and my 3 _ _ _ _ _ to honor Him.

I can use my 4 _ _ _ _ _ _ _ _ _ to help keep my body safe. I can 5 _ _ _ _ _ the sense of 6 _ _ _ _ _ _ _ with all my body parts.

Most people touch others in 7 _ _ _ _ _ ways, but sometimes people touch others in ways that feel 8 _ _ _ _ _ . 9 _ _ _ _ _ _ usually feel good, but sometimes they can feel bad.

I can say 10 "_ _ _ !" if someone tries to touch the 11 _ _ _ _ _ _ _ _ _ _ parts of my body or asks me to touch his or her 11 _ _ _ _ _ _ _ _ _ _ parts.

If my senses tell me that something could be wrong, I should try to 12 _ _ _ _ _ _ _ _ _ (two words).

If an adult tells me to keep a 13 _ _ _ _ _ _ _ about touching, I should 14 _ _ _ _ _ another adult that I trust.

If no one is around to help me when I have a problem, I can use a 15 _ _ _ _ _ _ _ _ _ to call for help.

cautious of the danger. On the other hand, do not overwhelm very young children with information that will frighten them.

Have your child read the first paragraph. Then read the story about Freddy while he colors the pictures. Ask him what three important things Freddy should do. *(1. Say "No." 2. Get away. 3. Tell someone.)* Discuss how Freddy can do each of these things.

First, Freddy should say in a confident way, "Coach, I don't like that kind of touching. Don't do that to me."

The second part, "getting away," will be difficult since Freddy and the coach are in a car. Discuss several possibilities with your child. If there are other people around, Freddy could try to jump out of the car and run and tell an adult that he needs help. He could say, "That man is trying to abuse me. Could you take me to a telephone so I can call my parents?" Then he should ask the adult to stay with him until his parents arrive. If there is no one around to tell, and there are no houses nearby, Freddy might be trapped and would need to try to convince the coach to take him home. In this case,

FREDDY'S PROBLEM

Most adults like children and do not want to harm them. But there are some people in the world who try to touch children in bad ways. Touching the private parts of a child's body is called *sexual abuse*. Read about one boy who had a problem with *sexual abuse*.

Freddy was a star player for the best Little League baseball team in town. Freddy could hit the ball farther, throw it harder, and run faster than anyone else on the team. Coach Charlie was excited to have such a good player on his team. Sometimes Coach Charlie picked up Freddy after school and took him to practice at a nearby park. Coach Charlie and Freddy's father were good friends, so Freddy's parents never worried about Freddy while he was with Coach Charlie.

One day after practice, Coach Charlie put his hand on Freddy's shoulder as he always did when they walked toward the car. "You are some ballplayer, Freddy. I'm going to buy you a special glove that will help you to play even better," he said.

"Wow!" exclaimed Freddy. He had wanted a new glove for a long time. This was too good to be true. "That's terrific, Coach. Do you really mean it?" he asked excitedly.

"Of course," smiled his coach as they got into the car. "We'll go over to the sporting goods store in a few minutes. But, first, I want to show you another way to have fun besides playing baseball. You are very special to me, Freddy. I like you a lot."

Then Coach Charlie gently put his hand inside Freddy's pants and touched his private parts.

Freddy just stared in surprise at Coach Charlie. He did not like this kind of touching, but he had always trusted Coach Charlie. He didn't want to hurt his feelings. Besides, Coach Charlie was going to buy him a new glove. But this kind of touching made him feel *yukky* inside. Freddy felt confused!

24

163

Freddy might have to say assertively, "Please don't do that. I don't like it. Please take me home." Discuss that the coach will probably ask him to keep it a secret. He should not tell the coach that he plans to tell his parents. Finally, discuss the possibility that the coach will not take him home and continues to abuse him. Freddy will have no choice at that point since the coach is too big to fight. *(Discourage false bravery such as "I'd give him a karate chop" under this circumstance.)* Assure your child that if this does happen, *it is the coach who did something wrong, not Freddy, and it is not Freddy's fault.*

The third point is that no matter what happened, even if Freddy promised the coach he would keep it a secret, he should tell his parents about the problem as soon as he gets home. If they don't believe him, he should tell another adult that he trusts as soon as possible. Discuss who Freddy could tell besides his parents.

After discussing the proper course of action, role play the situation, with your child pretending to be Freddy and you as Coach Charlie. *(Use a girl's*

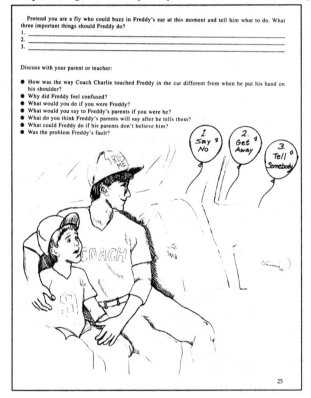

name if your daughter is uncomfortable playing a boy.) Do not role play the sexual abuse. Rather, begin with Freddy saying "No!" and carry through until Freddy's parents respond to his disclosure. *(Parents' response should be belief, expression of sadness that it happened, assurance that it wasn't Freddy's fault, and a promise to do something about it so that it never happens again.)*

Afterward, assure your child that if he ever has a problem similar to Freddy's, you want him to tell you right away. Remind him that it is wrong for an adult to abuse a child, and that you would do something about it if it happened to him.

End the lesson with lots of loving assurance that you hope your child never encounters a problem like this, but that you will believe him and take care of him if he does.

USE YOUR MIND TO HELP KEEP YOU SAFE

What would you do if you became separated from your parents at a busy shopping mall? Think about it while you color the picture below. Then write your answer on the lines below.

Pages 26-29
Objectives: To discuss a series of "What if?" situations with your child for an understanding about "stranger danger" and what she should do about specific problems; to expand the idea of "stranger danger" to an alertness about potential danger of abuse from someone she knows.
Understanding about personal body safety should evolve over a period of time. Do not expect your child to absorb it all at once.

For each page, have your child color while you talk comfortably and calmly about each situation. If you see your child becoming anxious, gently explore why. Reassure her that the lessons are intended to help keep her safe, not to frighten her. Do only one page at a time. Do not dwell on the subject after the lesson is over.

Page 26
Possible solutions when a child is separated from her parents:
● Tell a security officer or person wearing a uniform or name tag that you

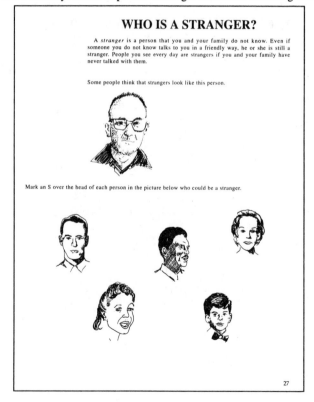

WHO IS A STRANGER?

A *stranger* is a person that you and your family do not know. Even if someone you do not know talks to you in a friendly way, he or she is still a stranger. People you see every day are strangers if you and your family have never talked with them.

Some people think that strangers look like this person.

Mark an S over the head of each person in the picture below who could be a stranger.

27

166

are lost.
- Stay in an area where there are people.
- Remain in the store or mall area where you became separated so your parents can come back and find you.
- Parents and older children can devise a plan to call a certain individual who can tell the parents where the child may be found. *(This plan needs a back-up in case the individual isn't home.)*

Discuss with your child exactly what you want her to do if she is ever separated from you.

Extra Activity: On your next trip to the mall, show your child where to go for help, the location of pay telephones, and the mall security office. Introduce her to a security guard, and tell her to ask a clerk to help her locate him if she is alone and in trouble. Rehearse your plan of action for separation.

TRUST YOUR BUILT-IN RADAR, YOUR SENSES, TO HELP YOU KNOW WHEN SOMETHING MIGHT BE WRONG

Most strangers do not want to harm children, but some do. Because of these few bad strangers, it's important to be careful around all strangers.

Something might be wrong when:

- a stranger asks you for information.
- a stranger wants to take your picture.
- a stranger asks you to help him/her find a lost pet.
- two friendly strangers drive up in a car and tell you your parents have asked them to bring you home.

28

167

Page 27

Discuss the definition of *stranger* printed at the top of the page. Mention specific individuals that your child may see in public places frequently and may think he knows simply because their faces are familiar *(store personnel, letter carrier, etc.)*. It is important that your child understands that a stranger's friendly face doesn't always mean he or she is friendly.

Page 28

To illustrate the first statement on the page, "Most strangers do not want to harm children," recall with your child seemingly nice strangers that you met together while in a store, restaurant, or other public place. Tell your child that these people probably would not do anything to hurt her. Unfortunately, though, bad strangers and good strangers look alike. It's often impossible to tell what a stranger might do just by the way he looks or acts. Therefore, tell your child that it is necessary that she not talk with anyone she does not know well when she is alone.

Ask your child to tell about a time when she sensed that something was wrong and found out that she was right. Stress again that our senses can help us detect danger. Encourage her to trust her senses when they tell her to be careful.

Discuss the situations of potential danger pictured on the page. In each case, ask your child to tell what she thinks is happening in each picture, what she thinks the stranger could do, and what she would do if she were the child in the picture. Expand on the basic rules: Say "No," get away, and tell someone.

(1) Teach your child that although it's good to help others, she should not feel obliged to help adults who are lost or are seeking information. Adults who need directions should ask other adults, not children. She could simply reply, "I'm sorry, I can't help you." She should try to remember what the stranger looked like, go on her way, and tell you what happened as soon as she reaches home. If a stranger asks information of a child playing in her own yard, she could reply, "Just a minute, I'll go get my mother (father)." Then she should come to get you to help the stranger.

Discuss the danger that a stranger might kidnap or abuse a child who tries to help him.

(2) Taking a child's picture could also be a kidnapping lure. Or the stranger might want a picture for identification for kidnapping by someone else. Instruct your child never to allow a stranger to take a photograph of him without your permission. A child's response to such an attempt could be, "I don't like to have my picture taken," and walk away immediately. As always, he should tell you right away.

(3) Molesters frequently engage children through gifts and pets. Appeal-

ing to a child's concern for a lost kitty or puppy is a common ploy. Warn your child not to be fooled by these kinds of traps.

(4) Teach your child never to get into a car or go with an adult unless you have given specific permission. Some parents use a family code word that no one else could know as proof that they have asked the adult to pick up their child. Sometimes this is such an intriguing mystery that a child may be tempted or tricked into divulging the code word. A better idea might be to develop together with your child a list of "trusted" adults that includes relatives, neighbors, friends, and teachers, that you could conceivably call upon in an emergency. Then make a blanket rule that your child is not to go with anyone other than these individuals.

Page 29

Children should be taught that indecent exposure is a form of sexual abuse.

Discuss with your child the two situations picture. Stress with him what he should do. For public exhibitionists, the child should try to remember the

individual's face and description, get away immediately, and tell an adult right away so the police can be called.

Situations of private exhibition may be more difficult for a child to deal with. The response is the same though: Say "No," go, and tell. Discuss how the child could do this if faced with such a problem at someone's home or in his own home.

Pages 30 and 31

Objective: To extend the "What if?" situations from "stranger danger" to abuse from someone who is known to your child.

As your child colors page 30, explain that sometimes teenagers as well as adults abuse children sexually. Stress that your child does not have to obey a baby-sitter who tells her to take off her clothes, touch private parts, look at dirty magazines, etc. If a baby-sitter ever tries anything like this with her, instruct your child to call you or a neighbor if possible. Discuss with your child what she should do if the baby-sitter prevents her from using the phone.

WHAT WOULD YOU DO IF . . .

. . . your baby-sitter showed you a magazine with pictures of people with no clothes on, hugged you, or promised you a nice surprise if you would take off your clothes?

30

In a similar way, discuss the situation at the neighbor's house pictured on page 31. Extend the concept of potential abuse to include any adult, even relatives.

Use your judgment to decide what additional "What if?" situations to discuss with your child.

- A friend wants her to hitchhike with her.
- Someone your child doesn't know is following him while he is walking alone.
- Someone tells her an off-color joke.
- He receives an obscene phone call.
- A stranger knocks at the door when she is alone.
- While sitting on someone's lap, the person touches her private parts.
- A trusted adult does something that makes him feel uncomfortable, then tells him not to tell anyone about it.

Review the assertive "no" response, the need to get away, pledging

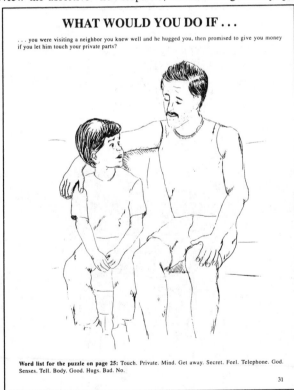

WHAT WOULD YOU DO IF . . .

. . . you were visiting a neighbor you knew well and he hugged you, then promised to give you money if you let him touch your private parts?

Word list for the puzzle on page 25: Touch. Private. Mind. Get away. Secret. Feel. Telephone. God. Senses. Tell. Body. Good. Hugs. Bad. No.

31

171

secrecy if necessary, and telling a trusted adult.

Discuss also what your child should do if another child tells her she has been abused, or if she sees another child in danger of abuse.

If you have not already done so, deal with a very real danger: No matter what your child may do to try to avoid abuse, it could still happen to her. Stress that if it does you will not blame her, and that she will not be in trouble. Include the possibility that she finds herself in an abusive situation after she broke a rule, such as going to the park alone. Assure her that you will help her, no matter what the circumstances or who the abuser is, and that you want her to tell you about it so it will not happen again.

Page 32
Objective: To culminate the lessons about personal body safety with the reassurance that most touches feel good, that God loves your child, and that he can feel happy knowing that God loves him.

Look up the Bible verse together. *(Answers: love, children, God.)* Then

GOD LOVES YOU AND WANTS YOU TO BE SAFE NO MATTER WHAT

"How great is the   the Father has lavished on us, that we should be called

of   ! And that is what we are!"   **–1 John 3:1**

sing songs together about God's love while your child colors the page. Song possibilities: "Jesus Loves Me," "God Is So Good," "His Banner Over Me Is Love." Pray together, thanking God for His love and goodness.

When you are done, just sit with your child in a way that expresses your love as you read a favorite story together!

Notes

1. Professor Jon Conte, Ph.D., University of Chicago, "Preventing the Sexual Molestation of Children," New York State Conference on Child Abuse and Neglect, April 21–24, 1985.

2. Anne Cohn, DPH, Director, National Committee for Prevention of Child Abuse, *An Approach to Preventing Child Abuse* (Chicago, NCPCA, 1981).

3. Gary May, MD, *Understanding Sexual Child Abuse* (Chicago, NCPCA, 1978), pp. 5-8.

4. Florence Rush, *The Best Kept Secret: Sexual Abuse of Children* (Englewood Cliffs, New Jersey, Prentice-Hall, Inc., 1980), pp. 48–55.

5. Dale Evans Rogers, *Hear the Children Crying: The Child Abuse Epidemic* (Charlotte, N.C., Commission Press, Inc., 1978), p. 21.

6. Rush, pp. 56–64.

7. *Ibid.*, pp. 80–104.

8. Jeffrey Masson, *The Assault on Truth: Freud's Suppression of the Seduction Theory*, 1984.

9. David Goleman, "New Insights Into Freud From Letters to a Friend" (New York Times Magazine, March 17, 1985.)

10. Rush, p. 187.

11. Vincent J. Fontana, MD, Medical Director, New York Foundling Hospital, *The Maltreated Child* (Illinois, Charles C. Thomas, Publisher, 1964).

12. Margaret O. Hyde, *Cry Softly: The Story of Child Abuse* (Philadelphia, The Westminster Press, 1985), pp. 58–60.

13. C. Henry Kempe, MD, and Ray E. Helfer, MD, eds., *The Battered Child* (Chicago, University of Chicago Press, 1968).

14. "Suffer the Children," *The Economist*, Jan. 27, 1990, p. 25.

15. D. Daro, and K. McCurdy, "Current Trends in Child Abuse Reporting and Fatalities: The Results of the 1991 Annual Fifty State Survey," *NCPCA Working Paper No. 808*, April 1992.

16. Douglas Besharov, "Protecting the Innocent," *National Review*, Feb. 19, 1990, p. 44.

17. D. Finklehor, L. Williams, and N. Burns, *Nursery Crimes: Sexual Abuse in Day Care*, 1988.

18. D. Daro, 1992.

19. *Ibid.*

20. *Ibid.*

21. Vincent Fontana, MD, *Save the Family, Save the Child*, 1991.

22. L. Mitchel, "Child Abuse and Neglect Fatalities: A Review of the Problem and Strategies for Reform," NCPCA, 1987.

23. D. Daro, 1992.

24. *Ibid.*

25. Paul Waller, "The Politics of Child Abuse," *Society*, V. 28 No. 6, Sept./Oct. 1991.

26. D. Daro, 1992.

27. "All Georgia Babies to have Cocaine Tests," *Chicago Tribune*, March 17, 1991.

28. A. Nicholas Groth, MD, Burgess, Holstrom, Sgroi, *Sexual Assault of Children and Adolescents* (Lexington, Mass., D.C. Heath & Co., 1980).

29. "Whose Responsibility Is It, Anyway?", *U.S. News and World Report*, Jan. 9, 1989, p. 29.

30. Flora Calao and Tamar Hosansky, *Your Children Should Know* (Indianapolis, The Bobbs-Merrill Company, Inc., 1983), p. 34.

31. Vincent DeFrancis, *Protecting the Child Victim of Sex Crimes Committed by Adults* (Denver, American Humane Association, 1969), p. 67.

32. Groth, pp. 6–11.

33. Judith Becker, Ph.D., Director, Sexual Behavior Clinic, NYS Psychiatric Clinic, "Treating Adolescent and Adult Sex Offenders," NY State Conference on Child Abuse and Neglect, April 21–24, 1985.

34. *Ibid.*

35. Groth, p. 4.

36. Suzanne Sgroi, MD, *Handbook of Clinical Intervention in Child Sexual Abuse* (Lexington, Mass., D.C. Heath Co., 1982), pp. 12–20.

37. Henry Giaretto, "A Comprehensive Sexual Abuse Treatment Program," in P.B. Mrazack and C.H. Kempe, eds., *Sexually Abused Children and Their Families* (Oxford, England, Pergamon Press, 1981).

38. Groth, p. 39.

39. Becker.

40. Fontana, *Save the Family, Save the Child*, 1991.

41. James C. Dobson, Ph.D., *Love Must Be Tough* (Waco, Texas, Word Publishers, 1983), pp. 154–156.

42. Sgroi, *Sexual Assault of Children and Adolescents*.

43. Dobson, *Love Must Be Tough*, pp. 154–156.

44. James Cameron, "Child Abuse and Neglect: Whose Problem? Whose Responsibility? A Decade of Evolving Ownership," (Albany, New York State Federation on Child Abuse and Neglect, 1985).

45. Flow chart copied from "A Guide to New York's Child Protection System," The New York State Assembly Select Committee on Child Abuse, Perry B. Duryea, Speaker, N.Y. State Assembly, Legislative Document No. 27, 1974.

46. "Suffer the Children," 1990, p. 25.

47. *Ibid.*

48. Sabdra Lee, "Should We Call the Police?" *McCall's*, May, 1991, p. 82.

49. D. Daro, 1992.

50. Mary H. Farrell, "Oprah's Crusade," *People*, Dec. 2, 1991, p. 69.

51. Douglas J. Besharov, "Building a Community Response to Child Abuse and Maltreatment," *Children Today*, Sept./Oct. 1975.
52. D. Daro, 1992.
53. Ellen Gray, Sophia Cohen, Michael Wald, "Preventing Child Maltreatment: A Review of What We Know," (NCPCA Working Paper No. 024, 1984).

Organizations Devoted to Child Abuse and Neglect Issues

American Humane Association, Children's Division, 63 Inverness Dr. E., Englewood, CO 80112, (303) 792–9900 or 1–800–227–5242.
Provides public information on nature and extent of child abuse through pamphlets, reports, and educational forums; promotes services to meet the needs of abused children, organizes new programs, and improves existing programs; provides help with community planning and training.

American Professional Society on the Abuse of Children, 332 S. Michigan Ave., Suite 1600, Chicago, IL 60604, (312) 554–0166.
APSAC is a multidisciplinary professional membership society founded to promote training, communication, and support among professionals who work with victims, survivors, families of victims, and perpetrators of child abuse.

American Red Cross
Local chapters provide training on child abuse and neglect for day care providers and others who work with children professionally.

Boys Town, 14100 Crawford St., Boys Town, NE 68010, (402) 498–1301.
Operates residential campuses for youth in eight states, a research hospital, a national training center, and family-based programs. National toll-free hotline for youth problems 1–800–448–3000.

Child Sexual Abuse Institute of Ohio, P.O. Box 453, Wooster, OH 44691, (216) 263–0579.
Provides counseling and therapy for sexual victims and their families and sexual offenders. Individual therapy, group therapy, retreats, training and consultation.

Childhelp U.S.A., Los Angeles, CA, 1–800–4–A–Child.
Toll-free number for assistance in crisis intervention, locating local agencies, providing resources, statistics.

Children's Defense Fund, 122 C St., N.W., Suite 400, Washington DC 20001, (202) 628–8787.
Addresses children's needs in the areas of income support, health, education, youth development, child care, child welfare, and mental health. Provides information and technical assistance and supports an annual federal legislative agenda.

Family Resource Coalition, 200 S. Michigan Ave., Suite 1520, Chicago, IL 60604, (312) 341–0900.
Membership of social service agencies concerned with strengthening families through preventive services; provides information on family resource programs, training sessions, and technical assistance.

Incest Survivors Anonymous, P.O. Box 5613, Long Beach, CA 90895–0613, (213) 422–1632.
Provides information on self-help meetings which are Twelve Step and Twelve-Tradition spiritually oriented for incest survivors.

Giaretto Institute, 232 E. Gish Rd., E., 1st Floor, San Jose, CA 95112, (408) 453–7616.
Services for victims including therapy, training offered for therapists and other professionals who work with abuse victims.

National Alliance of Children's Trust and Prevention Funds, 3908 Carlisle, N.E., Albuquerque, NM 87107, (505) 881–4545.

National Center for the Prevention and Treatment of Child Abuse and Neglect, 1205 Oneida St., Denver, CO 80220, (303) 321–3963.
Develops treatment programs for abused children, provides training and technical assistance.

National Center on Child Abuse and Neglect, Administration for Children and Families, U.S. Dept. of Health and Human Services, P.O. Box 1182, Washington, DC 20013, (202) 245–0814.
Conducts research and disseminates information, provides assistance to states and communities on the prevention, identification and treatment of child abuse and neglect. For information contact the NCCAN Clearinghouse for professionals (703) 385–7565.

National Child Abuse Hotline
For information and referral, 1–800–422–4453.

National Committee for Prevention of Child Abuse, 332 S. Michigan Ave., Suite 1600, Chicago, IL 60604, (312) 663–3520.

Coordinating body for state chapters and other organizations devoted to the prevention of child abuse and neglect; promotes public awareness of child abuse and neglect issues through the media, conferences, and publications with a special emphasis on prevention programs and parenting education; catalog of publications available upon request. Comprehensive booklet of child sexual abuse prevention resources.

National Court Appointed Special Advocates Association, 2722 Eastlake Ave., East, Suite 220, Seattle, WA 98102, (206) 328–8588.
Supports and develops local CASA (Court Appointed Special Advocate) programs to train community volunteers for appointment by local judges to speak up for abused and neglected children in court as well as to follow a particular case from start to finish as a consistent support person for the victim.

National Parent Aide Association, 322 S. Michigan Ave., Suite 1600, Chicago, IL 60604, (312) 663–3520.
Supports parent aide programs by providing resources for local programs. Publishes a directory listing over 200 programs nationwide.

National Resource Center on Child Sexual Abuse, 106 Lincoln St., Huntsville, AL 35801, 1–800–543–7006.
Provides services for professionals working in the field of child sexual abuse — training, referral, consultation, prosecution.

Parents Anonymous (P.A.), 520 S. Lafayette Park Place, Suite 316, Los Angeles, CA 90057, 1–800–421–0353.
Self-help international organization with over 1500 chapters for parents under stress; also works with abused children.

Parents United International, 232 E. Gish Rd., 1st Floor, San Jose, CA 95112, (408) 453–7616.
Provides assistance to adults who were sexually abused as children and to their families. Chapters work with a sponsoring agency to provide professionally led group therapy by licensed counselors.

PACER Center, 4826 Chicago Ave., S., Minneapolis, MN 55417, (612) 827–2966.
Project provides puppet shows, workshops, and written materials to groups and parent organizations about child maltreatment and increased vulnerability for disabled children.

Salvation Army
Call local chapters for emergency shelter, temporary foster care, counsel-

ing, care and guidance for children or parents in need.

The Spiritual Dimension in Victim Services, 2700 L Street, Sacramento, CA 95816, (916) 446-7202.
Provides training for clergy, communities, and victim assistance providers. Specializes in serving the religious community.

United Way
Local chapters can provide information about agencies in your community who provide information or services relating to child abuse and neglect.

VOICES in Action, Inc., P.O. Box 148309, Chicago, IL 60614, (312) 327-1500.
Provides referrals to self-help and therapy resources for victims of incest.